.

FIRST NAME

SURNAME

HOME ADDRESS (LINE 1)

HOME ADDRESS (LINE 2)

HOME PHONE

MOBILE PHONE

EMAIL

TWITTER

INSTAGRAM

BUSINESS/COLLEGE ADDRESS (LINE 1)

BUSINESS/COLLEGE ADDRESS (LINE 2)

BUSINESS/COLLEGE PHONE

BUSINESS/COLLEGE EMAIL

EMERGENCY CONTACT (NAME AND PHONE NUMBER)

BLOOD GROUP

ALLERGIES

VACCINATIONS

PASSPORT NO.

PASSPORT EXPIRY DATE

DRIVER'S LICENSE NO.

UK BANK HOLIDAYS

JANUARY 1ST — New Year's Day

APRIL 19TH — Good Friday

APRIL 22ND — Easter Monday

MAY 6TH — Early May Bank Holiday

MAY 27TH — Spring Bank Holiday

AUGUST 26TH — Summer Bank Holiday

DECEMBER 25TH — Christmas Day

DECEMBER 26TH — Boxing Day

US FEDERAL HOLIDAYS

JANUARY 1ST — New Year's Day

JANUARY 21ST — Martin Luther King Day

FEBRUARY 18TH — Presidents' Day

MAY 27TH — Memorial Day

JULY 4TH — Independence Day

SEPTEMBER 2ND — Labor Day

OCTOBER 14TH — Indigenous Peoples' Day

NOVEMBER 11TH — Veterans Day

NOVEMBER 28TH — Thanksgiving Day

DECEMBER 25TH — Christmas Day

Verso Books is the largest independent,
radical publishing house in the English-speaking world.

Launched by New Left Review in 1970, Verso
is a leading publisher in current affairs, philosophy,
history, politics and economics.

"A rigorously intelligent publisher."
—SUNDAY TIMES

"Anglo-America's preeminent radical press."
—HARPER'S

VERSOBOOKS.COM

Buy securely and easily from our website—
great discounts, free shipping with a minimum order
and a free ebook bundled with many of our hard-copy books.

Check our website to read our blog and see our latest
titles—featuring essays, videos, podcasts,
interviews with authors, news, exclusive competitions
and details of forthcoming events.

Sign up to our email list to be the first to hear of
our new titles, special offers and events.

@VersoBooks

versobooks.tumblr.com

Verso Books

versobooks

Some of the quotes in the calendar are drawn
from *The Verso Book of Dissent*, edited by
Andrew Hsiao and Audrea Lim (Verso 2016).

2019

JANUARY

S	M	T	W	TH	F	S
30	31	1	2	3	4	5
6	7	8	9	10	11	12
13	14	15	16	17	18	19
20	21	22	23	24	25	26
27	28	29	30	31	1	2

FEBRUARY

S	M	T	W	TH	F	S
27	28	29	30	31	1	2
3	4	5	6	7	8	9
10	11	12	13	14	15	16
17	18	19	20	21	22	23
24	25	26	27	28	1	2

MARCH

S	M	T	W	TH	F	S
24	25	26	27	28	1	2
3	4	5	6	7	8	9
10	11	12	13	14	15	16
17	18	19	20	21	22	23
24	25	26	27	28	29	30
31						

APRIL

S	M	T	W	TH	F	S
31	1	2	3	4	5	6
7	8	9	10	11	12	13
14	15	16	17	18	19	20
21	22	23	24	25	26	27
28	29	30	1	2	3	4

MAY

S	M	T	W	TH	F	S
28	29	30	1	2	3	4
5	6	7	8	9	10	11
12	13	14	15	16	17	18
19	20	21	22	23	24	25
26	27	28	29	30	31	1

JUNE

S	M	T	W	TH	F	S
26	27	28	29	30	31	1
2	3	4	5	6	7	8
9	10	11	12	13	14	15
16	17	18	19	20	21	22
23	24	25	26	27	28	29
30						

JULY

S	M	T	W	TH	F	S
30	1	2	3	4	5	6
7	8	9	10	11	12	13
14	15	16	17	18	19	20
21	22	23	24	25	26	27
28	29	30	31	1	2	3

AUGUST

S	M	T	W	TH	F	S
28	29	30	31	1	2	3
4	5	6	7	8	9	10
11	12	13	14	15	16	17
18	19	20	21	22	23	24
25	26	27	28	29	30	31

SEPTEMBER

S	M	T	W	TH	F	S
1	2	3	4	5	6	7
8	9	10	11	12	13	14
15	16	17	18	19	20	21
22	23	24	25	26	27	28
29	30	1	2	3	4	5

OCTOBER

S	M	T	W	TH	F	S
29	30	1	2	3	4	5
6	7	8	9	10	11	12
13	14	15	16	17	18	19
20	21	22	23	24	25	26
27	28	29	30	31	1	2

NOVEMBER

S	M	T	W	TH	F	S
27	28	29	30	31	1	2
3	4	5	6	7	8	9
10	11	12	13	14	15	16
17	18	19	20	21	22	23
24	25	26	27	28	29	30

DECEMBER

S	M	T	W	TH	F	S
1	2	3	4	5	6	7
8	9	10	11	12	13	14
15	16	17	18	19	20	21
22	23	24	25	26	27	28
29	30	31	1	2	3	4

2020

JANUARY

S	M	T	W	TH	F	S
29	30	31	1	2	3	4
5	6	7	8	9	10	11
12	13	14	15	16	17	18
19	20	21	22	23	24	25
26	27	28	29	30	31	1

FEBRUARY

S	M	T	W	TH	F	S
26	27	28	29	30	31	1
2	3	4	5	6	7	8
9	10	11	12	13	14	15
16	17	18	19	20	21	22
23	24	25	26	27	28	29

MARCH

S	M	T	W	TH	F	S
1	2	3	4	5	6	7
8	9	10	11	12	13	14
15	16	17	18	19	20	21
22	23	24	25	26	27	28
29	30	31	1	2	3	4

APRIL

S	M	T	W	TH	F	S
29	30	31	1	2	3	4
5	6	7	8	9	10	11
12	13	14	15	16	17	18
19	20	21	22	23	24	25
26	27	28	29	30	1	2

MAY

S	M	T	W	TH	F	S
26	27	28	29	30	1	2
3	4	5	6	7	8	9
10	11	12	13	14	15	16
17	18	19	20	21	22	23
24	25	26	27	28	29	30
31						

JUNE

S	M	T	W	TH	F	S
31	1	2	3	4	5	6
7	8	9	10	11	12	13
14	15	16	17	18	19	20
21	22	23	24	25	26	27
28	29	30	1	2	3	4

JULY

S	M	T	W	TH	F	S
28	29	30	1	2	3	4
5	6	7	8	9	10	11
12	13	14	15	16	17	18
19	20	21	22	23	24	25
26	27	28	29	30	31	1

AUGUST

S	M	T	W	TH	F	S
26	27	28	29	30	31	1
2	3	4	5	6	7	8
9	10	11	12	13	14	15
16	17	18	19	20	21	22
23	24	25	26	27	28	29
30	31					

SEPTEMBER

S	M	T	W	TH	F	S
30	31	1	2	3	4	5
6	7	8	9	10	11	12
13	14	15	16	17	18	19
20	21	22	23	24	25	26
27	28	29	30	1	2	3

OCTOBER

S	M	T	W	TH	F	S
27	28	29	30	1	2	3
4	5	6	7	8	9	10
11	12	13	14	15	16	17
18	19	20	21	22	23	24
25	26	27	28	29	30	31

NOVEMBER

S	M	T	W	TH	F	S
1	2	3	4	5	6	7
8	9	10	11	12	13	14
15	16	17	18	19	20	21
22	23	24	25	26	27	28
29	30	1	2	3	4	5

DECEMBER

S	M	T	W	TH	F	S
29	30	1	2	3	4	5
6	7	8	9	10	11	12
13	14	15	16	17	18	19
20	21	22	23	24	25	26
27	28	29	30	31	1	2

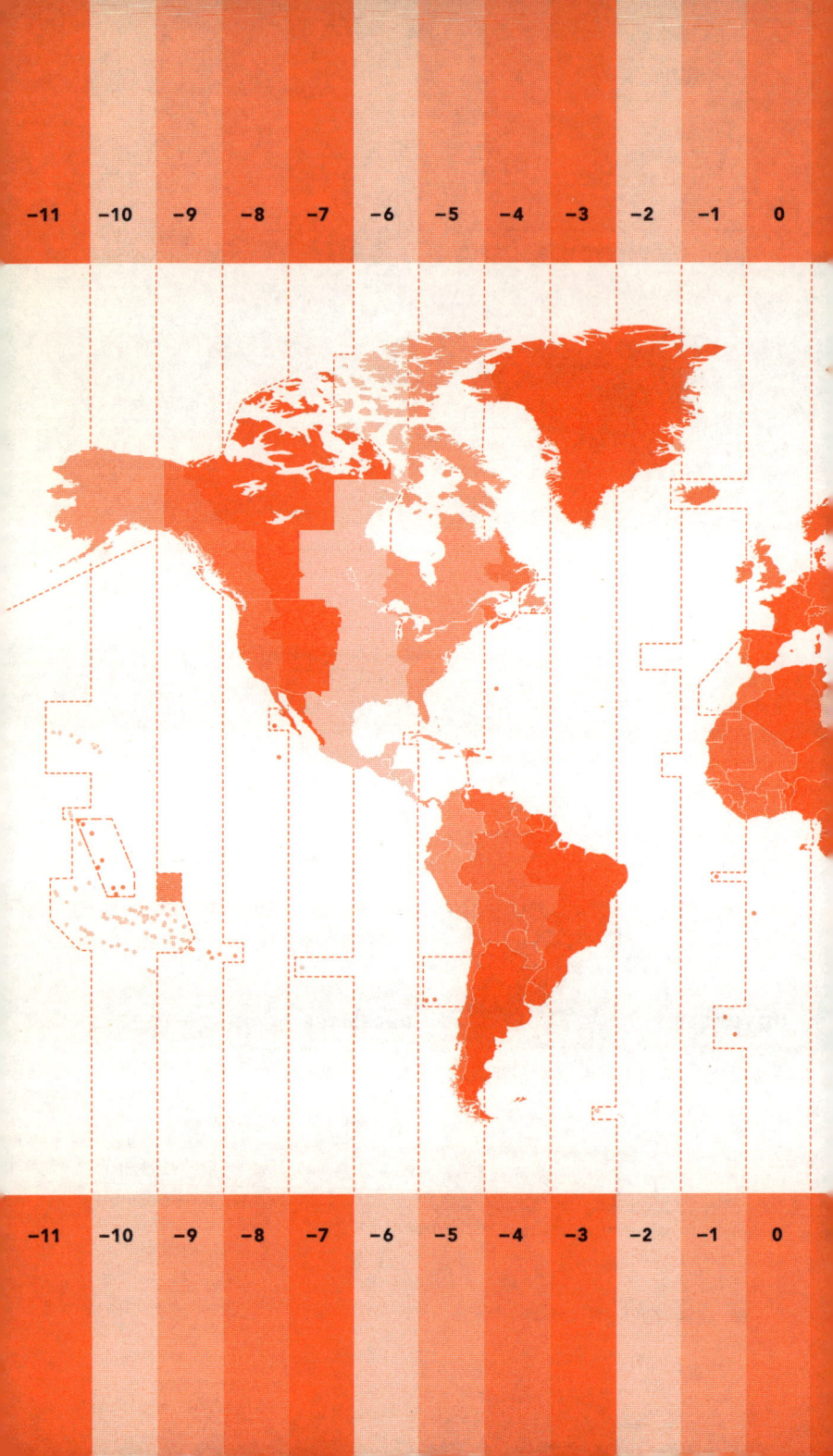

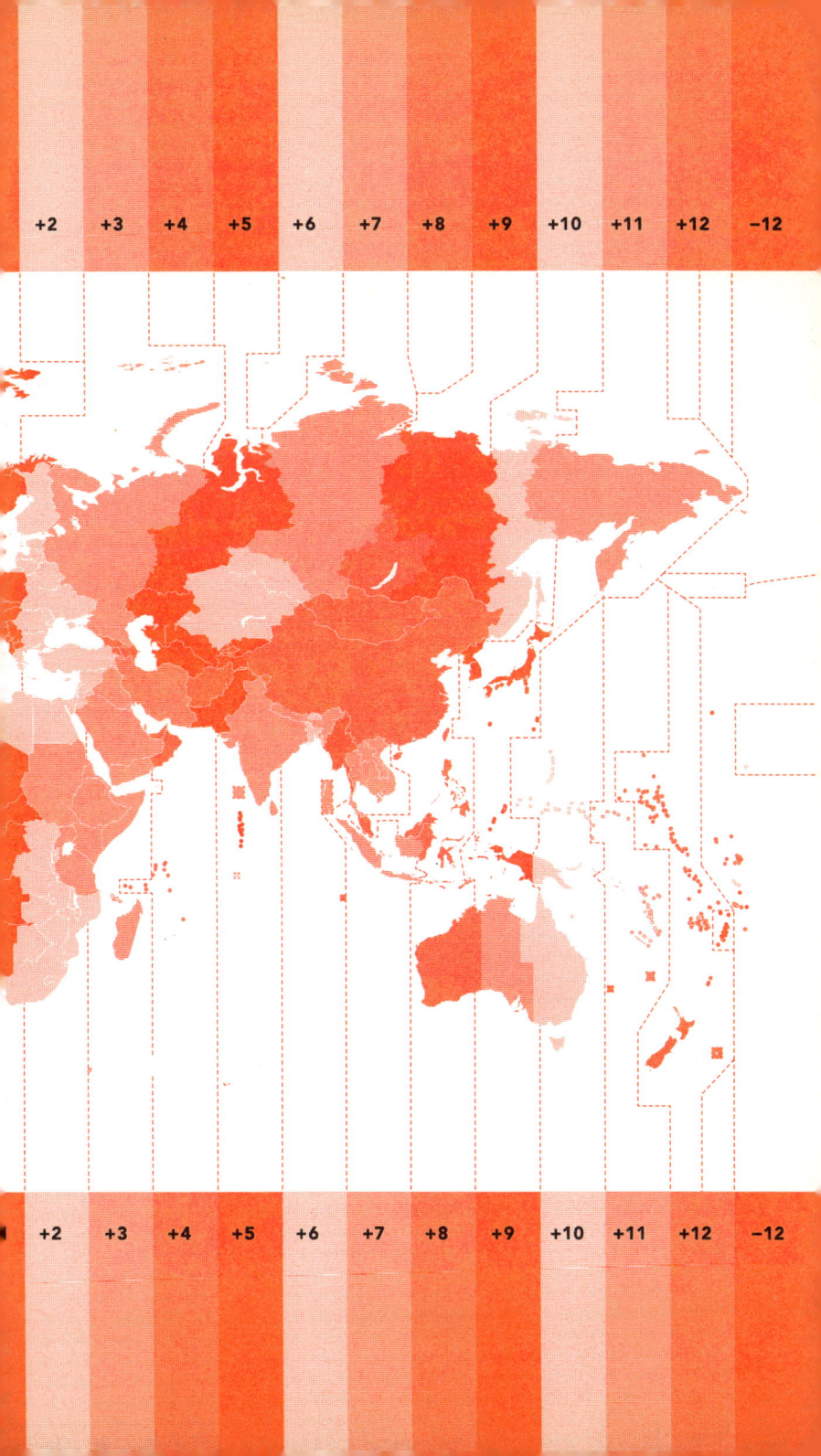

MONDAY DECEMBER 31

TUESDAY JANUARY 1

WEDNESDAY JANUARY 2

JANUARY 1, 1994 Zapatista forces overtake towns in Chiapas, beginning an ongoing revolution against the Mexican state. "The dispossessed, we are millions, and we thereby call upon our brothers and sisters to join this struggle as the only path." **—ZAPATISTA ARMY OF NATIONAL LIBERATION**

JANUARY 1, 2009 Oscar Grant III was a twenty-two-year-old black man, fatally shot by an Oakland, California, transit cop in the early morning hours of the New Year. The riots that followed were some of the largest the United States had seen in decades. "Oscar Grant: Murdered. The Whole Damn System Is Guilty!" **—PLACARD FROM THE OSCAR GRANT REBELLION**

JANUARY 3, 1961 Angolan peasants employed by the Portuguese-Belgium cotton plantation company Cotonang begin protests over poor working conditions, setting off the Angolan struggle for independence from Portugal.

"Tomorrow we will sing songs of freedom
    when we commemorate
    the day this slavery ends."

—FIRST PRESIDENT OF ANGOLA AND LEADER OF THE MOVEMENT FOR THE LIBERATION OF ANGOLA ANTONIO AGOSTINHO NETO, "FAREWELL AT THE HOUR OF PARTING"

JANUARY 5, 1971 Angela Davis—black feminist, philosopher, and prison abolitionist—declares her innocence in a California court over the kidnapping and murder of a judge. "Prisons do not disappear problems, they disappear human beings. And the practice of disappearing vast numbers of people from poor, immigrant, and racially marginalized communities has literally become big business." **—"MASKED RACISM"**

JANUARY 6, 1977 Charter 77, a document criticizing the Czech government for its human rights record, is published; it is violently suppressed.

THURSDAY JANUARY 3

Subcomandante Marcos and Comandante Tacho in La Realidad, Chiapas, 1999

FRIDAY JANUARY 4

NOTES:

SATURDAY JANUARY 5

SUNDAY JANUARY 6

MONDAY JANUARY 7

TUESDAY JANUARY 8

WEDNESDAY JANUARY 9

JANUARY 7, 1957 Djamila Bouhired, the "Arab Joan of Arc" and member of the National Liberation Front, sets off a bomb in an Algiers café, precipitating the Battle of Algiers, a pivotal episode in the Algerian struggle for independence against the French. "It was the most beautiful day of my life because I was confident that I was going to be dying for the sake of the most wonderful story in the world."

JANUARY 9, 1959 Rigoberta Menchú Tum, indigenous revolutionary and Nobel Peace Prize winner, is born in Chimel, Guatemala. "[My cause] wasn't born out of something good, it was born out of wretchedness and bitterness. It has been radicalized by the poverty in which my people live." —*I, RIGOBERTA MENCHÚ*

JANUARY 10, 1776 Thomas Paine, who participated in the American and French revolutions, publishes the pamphlet *Common Sense*, which argued for American independence from Britain. "Society in every state is a blessing, but government even in its best state is but a necessary evil; in its worst state an intolerable one."

JANUARY 11, 1894 Donghak Rebellion begins in Mujiang, Korea, over local corruption, eventually growing into an anti-establishment movement. "The people are the root of the nation. If the root withers, the nation will be enfeebled." —DONGHAK REBELLION PROCLAMATION

JANUARY 11, 1912 Workers in Lawrence, Massachusetts, walk out over a race-based pay cut in what would become known as the "bread and roses" strike. Soon an Industrial Workers of the World–organized strike shuts down every textile mill in the city.

"As we come marching, marching, we bring the greater days.
The rising of the women means the rising of the race."
    —LAWRENCE STRIKERS

THURSDAY JANUARY 10

Strikers face the Massachusetts State Militia, 1912

FRIDAY JANUARY 11

NOTES:

SATURDAY JANUARY 12

SUNDAY JANUARY 13

MONDAY JANUARY 14

TUESDAY JANUARY 15

WEDNESDAY JANUARY 16

JANUARY 15, 1919 Rosa Luxemburg, founder of the Spartacus League, is murdered by the German Social Democratic government. "The madness will cease and the bloody demons of hell will vanish only when workers in Germany and France, England and Russia finally awake from their stupor, extend to each other a brotherly hand, and drown out the bestial chorus of imperialist war-mongers." *—JUNIUS PAMPHLET*

JANUARY 17, 1893 Queen Lili'uokalani, Hawaii's last monarch, is overthrown by American colonists.

JANUARY 17, 1961 Patrice Lumumba, Congolese independence leader and first prime minister of independent Congo, is assassinated by the Belgian government. Six months earlier, he had been deposed in a CIA-backed coup. "They are trying to distort your focus when they call our government a communist government, in the pay of the Soviet Union, or say that Lumumba is a communist, an anti-white: Lumumba is an African."

JANUARY 20, 1973 Amílcar Cabral, a communist intellectual and guerrilla leader of Guinea-Bissau's anti-colonial movement against the Portuguese, is assassinated. Guinea-Bissau became independent just months later. "Honesty, in a political context, is total commitment and total identification with the toiling masses."

JANUARY 20, 2017 Hundreds of protesters are arrested in Washington, DC as Donald Trump is inaugurated as US president, and the following day, an estimated 470,000 people rally for the Women's March on Washington. "Pussy Grabs Back." **—PROTEST SLOGAN**

THURSDAY JANUARY 17

Patrice Lumumba (1925–1961) raises his unshackled arms following his release, 1960

FRIDAY JANUARY 18

NOTES:

SATURDAY JANUARY 19

SUNDAY JANUARY 20

MONDAY JANUARY 21

TUESDAY JANUARY 22

WEDNESDAY JANUARY 23

JANUARY 21, 1935 The Wilderness Society is founded by conservationists; it would become one of the most radical US environmentalist groups into the 1970s. "Our bigger-and-better society is now like a hypochondriac, so obsessed with its own economic health as to have lost the capacity to remain healthy." —SOCIETY FOUNDER ALDO LEOPOLD, *A SAND COUNTY ALMANAC*

JANUARY 22, 1936 Burmese student union leaders Aung San and U Nu are expelled for criticizing British rule in Burma, leading to a national student strike. "Escaped from Awizi a devil in the form of a black dog ... Will finder please kick him back to hell." —NYO MYA, "A HELL HOUND AT LARGE"

JANUARY 22, 2006 Evo Morales, first indigenous president of Bolivia, is sworn into office.

JANUARY 23, 1976 Paul Robeson, the African-American singer and civil rights campaigner, dies. "I stand always on the side of those who will toil and labor. As an artist I come to sing, but as a citizen, I will always speak for peace, and no one can silence me in this."

JANUARY 24, 1911 The anarcho-feminist Kanno Sugako is hanged for plotting to assassinate Emperor Meiji. "In accordance with long-standing customs, we have been seen as a form of material property. Women in Japan are in a state of slavery." —"WOMEN ARE SLAVES"

JANUARY 27, 1924 Lenin's funeral takes place in Red Square. In attendance was the poet Vladimir Mayakovsky, who went on to pen the epic poem, "Vladimir Ilyich Lenin."

"Just guzzling
        snoozing
                and pocketing pelf,
    Capitalism
        got lazy and feeble."

THURSDAY JANUARY 24

Activist, singer, and actor Paul Robeson (1898–1976)

FRIDAY JANUARY 25

NOTES:

SATURDAY JANUARY 26

SUNDAY JANUARY 27

MONDAY JANUARY 28

_____

_____

_____

_____

_____

_____

_____

_____

TUESDAY JANUARY 29

_____

_____

_____

_____

_____

_____

_____

_____

WEDNESDAY JANUARY 30

_____

_____

_____

_____

_____

_____

_____

_____

JANUARY 28, 1948 A plane crash kills twenty-eight bracero farm workers being sent back to Mexico. Cesar Chavez considered the moment part of his early political education.

> "Who are all these friends, all scattered like dry leaves?
> The radio says, 'They are just deportees ...'"
> **—WOODY GUTHRIE, "DEPORTEE"**

JANUARY 29, 1967 Arusha Declaration, written by Julius Nyerere, is issued to clarify Tanzania's path toward Ujamaa, or African socialism. "We, in Africa, have no more need of being 'converted' to socialism than we have of being 'taught' democracy." **—"UJAMAA, THE BASIS OF AFRICAN SOCIALISM"**

JANUARY 30, 1972 British soldiers shot twenty-eight unarmed civilians in Northern Ireland during a peaceful protest march against internment, in what become known as Bloody Sunday—one of the most significant brutal events of The Troubles.

FEBRUARY 1, 1902 Langston Hughes, poet and figure of the Harlem Renaissance, is born.

> "What happens to a dream deferred?
> Does it dry up
> like a raisin in the sun?
> Or fester like a sore—
> and then run?"
> **—"MONTAGE OF A DREAM DEFERRED"**

FEBRUARY 2, 1512 Taíno hero Hatuey is captured and killed after besieging the Spaniards for four months at their first fort in Cuba. "[Gold] is the God the Spaniards worship. For these they fight and kill, for these they persecute us and that is why we have to throw them into the sea." **—HATUEY'S SPEECH TO THE TAÍNOS**

FEBRUARY 3, 1930 The Indochinese Communist Party is established; it conducted an underground struggle against the French colonialists and, later, the American invaders.

THURSDAY JANUARY 31

Torture of Hatuey in Cuba, by Theodor de Bry, 1590

FRIDAY FEBRUARY 1

NOTES:

SATURDAY FEBRUARY 2

SUNDAY FEBRUARY 3

FRANTZ FANON
ELAINE MOKHTEFI

Frantz Fanon was born and raised on the West Indian island of Martinique, then a French overseas department (a territory whose relation to France was on the order of Puerto Rico's to the United States). During the Second World War, Fanon managed to escape the island's Vichy regime to enlist with de Gaulle's Free French Forces. He was shipped to North Africa, where he received his first impressions of colonial Algeria while awaiting transfer to Europe. Wounded in action at Colmar near the German border, he was awarded the Croix de Guerre. He returned to Martinique in 1945, finished high school, then left for Lyon, France, where he entered medical school, specializing in psychiatry.

After the war for independence broke out in November 1954, Fanon came into contact with the Algerian National Liberation Army and began providing medical and psychiatric aid, as well as shelter, to the freedom fighters. In 1956 he resigned from his medical post. In an open letter addressed to Robert Lacoste, the resident general of Algeria, he declared:

> If psychiatry is the medical technique that aims to enable man no longer to be a stranger in his own environment, I affirm that the Arab, permanent alien in his own country, lives in a state of absolute depersonalization. The events in Algeria are the logical consequence of an abortive attempt to decerebrate a people.

Lacoste subsequently deported Fanon from Algeria. So the doctor and his family made their way to Tunis, where he joined the Algerian provisional government headquarters and immersed himself in a variety of roles: as staff writer at *El Moudjahid*, the FLN

newspaper, and as psychiatrist and head of a day clinic for Algerian freedom fighters and war victims. He lectured to officers of the Algerian National Liberation Army at Ghardimaou on the Algeria–Tunisia border.

Fanon's rise in the Algerian hierarchy was phenomenal—especially considering that he was neither Algerian-born or raised, nor was he Muslim. In December 1958, Fanon headed the Algerian delegation to the All-African People's Conference in Accra, a short-lived but politically powerful organization. It was there that he met and developed close relationships with Patrice Lumumba from the Congo, Holden Roberto (alias Rui Ventura) of Angola, and Félix Moumié of Cameroon. In 1959, he was named the first Algerian ambassador to Ghana. It was there that I met him.

Fanon had a long face, a strong, wide jaw, and deep-set, probing eyes. He was short, his body taut. The overall picture was of intensity, a man in a hurry and driven. As an official observer at the WAY congress, Fanon was invited to address the delegates.

One night Fanon and I went dancing. A Ghanaian photographer focused his camera on us. Frantz caught him on the edge of the dance floor, and warned him to destroy the photo (it appeared nonetheless in an Accra newspaper a few days later). The FLN had placed a boycott on all French cigarettes. When I shared my Gauloises with him, we became partners in guilt, breaking the ban together.

He once asked me what I wanted in a relationship. When I answered, "To put my head on someone's shoulder," he was adamant: "Non, non, non: stay upright on your own two feet and keep moving forward to goals of your own." His words would come back to me often, and I have repeated them to others in need of that advice, as I was at the time.

This is a revised extract from Elaine Mokhtefi's Algiers, Third World Capital: Freedom Fighters, Revolutionaries, Black Panthers *(Verso, 2018).*

MONDAY FEBRUARY 4

FEBRUARY 4, 1899 Philippine-American war begins after the Philippine government objects to being handed over to the US from Spain.

> "The North
> Americans have
> captured nothing
> but a vessel
> of water,
> nothing that
> our sun
> will find difficult
> to empty with its rage."
> —ALFREDO NAVARRO SALANGA

TUESDAY FEBRUARY 5

FEBRUARY 7, 1948 Tens of thousands of silent marchers in Bogotá memorialize victims of Colombian state violence. "Señor Presidente, our flag is in mourning; this silent multitude, the mute cry from our hearts, asks only that you treat us ... as you would have us treat you." —JORGE ELIÉCER GAITÁN, LEADER OF THE COLOMBIAN LIBERAL PARTY

FEBRUARY 8, 1677 Andrew Marvell, English poet and parliamentarian during the Anglo-Dutch wars, publishes his last known work. "There has now for divers years a design been carried on to change the lawful government of England into an absolute tyranny." —AN ACCOUNT OF THE GROWTH OF POPERY AND ARBITRARY GOVERNMENT IN ENGLAND

WEDNESDAY FEBRUARY 6

FEBRUARY 8, 1996 John Perry Barlow publishes "A Declaration of the Independence of Cyberspace" in response to an anti-pornography bill passed by the US Congress that would have chilled online speech dramatically. "On behalf of the future, I ask you of the past to leave us alone."

FEBRUARY 10, 1883 The Russian revolutionary Vera Figner is arrested for her role in Tsar Alexander II's assassination. She received a death sentence that was later commuted. "My past experience had convinced me that the only way to change the existing order was by force." —MEMOIRS OF A REVOLUTIONIST

THURSDAY FEBRUARY 7

Vera Nikolayevna Figner (1852–1942) after the 1905 Russian Revolution

FRIDAY FEBRUARY 8

NOTES:

SATURDAY FEBRUARY 9

SUNDAY FEBRUARY 10

MONDAY FEBRUARY 11

TUESDAY FEBRUARY 12

WEDNESDAY FEBRUARY 13

FEBRUARY 11, 1916 Emma Goldman, anarchist agitator, publisher and all-around "rebel woman," is arrested for distributing a pamphlet about birth control written by Margaret Sanger.

FEBRUARY 11, 1990 Nelson Mandela is freed after twenty-seven years as a political prisoner. Four years later he became the first president of post-apartheid South Africa.

FEBRUARY 12, 1919 Subhash Mukhopadhyay, the leading Bengali communist poet of the twentieth century, is born.

"Who are those who fasten on the walls
The manifesto of an unborn day?"
  —"FOR A POEM"

FEBRUARY 13, 1967 Forough Farrokhzad, feminist poet who has inspired much debate in Iran about modernity, dies in a car crash.

"If you want these bonds broken,
  grasp the skirt of obstinacy."
    —"CALL TO ARMS"

FEBRUARY 14, 1818 The birth date chosen by Frederick Douglass, America's foremost abolitionist writer and activist. "What, to the American slave, is your 4th of July? I answer: a day that reveals to him, more than all other days in the year, the gross injustice and cruelty to which he is the constant victim." **—"THE MEANING OF JULY FOURTH FOR THE NEGRO"**

FEBRUARY 15, 1855 Muktabai, a fourteen-year-old Dalit, publishes the earliest surviving piece of writing by an "untouchable" woman. "Let that religion, where only one person is privileged and the rest are deprived, perish from the earth and let it never enter our minds to be proud of such a religion." **—"ABOUT THE GRIEFS OF THE MANGS AND MAHARS"**

FEBRUARY 17, 1958 The Campaign for Nuclear Disarmament is founded in Britain; it would become the country's most important protest movement during the late 1950s and early 1960s.

THURSDAY FEBRUARY 14

Abolitionist and ex-slave Frederick Douglass (1818–1895)

FRIDAY FEBRUARY 15

NOTES:

SATURDAY FEBRUARY 16

SUNDAY FEBRUARY 17

MONDAY FEBRUARY 18

_____

_____

_____

_____

_____

_____

_____

TUESDAY FEBRUARY 19

_____

_____

_____

_____

_____

_____

_____

WEDNESDAY FEBRUARY 20

_____

_____

_____

_____

_____

_____

_____

_____

FEBRUARY 18, 1934 Black lesbian poet Audre Lorde is born in New York City.

"For all of us
this instant and this triumph
We were never meant to survive."
—**"A LITANY FOR SURVIVAL"**

FEBRUARY 19, 1942 Japanese American internment begins in the US through Executive Order 9066.

FEBRUARY 19, 1963 Betty Friedan's _The Feminine Mystique_, a classic of second-wave feminism, is published. "The problem lay buried, unspoken, for many years in the minds of American women."

FEBRUARY 21, 1848 The _Communist Manifesto_, written by Friedrich Engels and Karl Marx, is published. "The proletarians have nothing to lose but their chains. They have a world to win."

FEBRUARY 21, 1965 Malcolm X is assassinated at the Audubon Ballroom in New York City. "Uncle Sam's hands are dripping with blood, dripping with the blood of the black man in this country." —**"THE BALLOT OR THE BULLET"**

FEBRUARY 23, 1848 French revolutionaries overthrow the Orléans monarchy and establish the Second Republic, where socialist Louis Blanc attempts to implement worker cooperatives. "What does competition mean to working men? It is the distribution of work to the highest bidder." —**"THE ORGANIZATION OF LABOUR"**

FEBRUARY 23, 1934 George Padmore, leading Pan-Africanist born in Trinidad, is expelled from the Comintern and shifts his focus to African independence struggles. "The black man certainly has to pay dear for carrying the white man's burden." —**"THE WHITE MAN'S BURDEN"**

THURSDAY FEBRUARY 21

Malcolm X (1925–1965) by Ed Ford, World Telegram staff photographer

FRIDAY FEBRUARY 22

NOTES:

SATURDAY FEBRUARY 23

SUNDAY FEBRUARY 24

MONDAY FEBRUARY 25

TUESDAY FEBRUARY 26

WEDNESDAY FEBRUARY 27

FEBRUARY 26, 1906 Upton Sinclair's exposé on the meat packing industry, *The Jungle*, is published, prompting the enactment of the Meat Inspection and Pure Food and Drug Acts.

FEBRUARY 27, 1832 Auguste Blanqui, French revolutionary and early theorist of class struggle, is found guilty (with fourteen others) of supporting republicanism. "This is the war between the rich and the poor: the rich wanted it so, for they are the aggressors. But they find it wrong that the poor fight back." —BLANQUI'S DEFENSE SPEECH

FEBRUARY 27, 1973 Oglala Lakota and American Indian Movement members, including Leonard Peltier, begin an occupation of Wounded Knee, South Dakota on the Pine Ridge Indian Reservation.

MARCH 1, 1896 Ethiopian fighters defeat Italian forces at the Battle of Adwa, securing Ethiopian sovereignty to become a symbol of African resistance against European colonialism. "Once a white snake has bitten you, you will find no cure for it." —ETHIOPIAN REBEL LEADER BAHTA HAGOS

MARCH 1, 1940 Richard Wright's seminal novel *Native Son*, about a black youth living on Chicago's South Side, is published. His writings would shift the US discourse on race.

"FB eye under my bed
Told me all I dreamed last night, every word I said."
—"FB EYE BLUES"

MARCH 1, 1954 Lolita Lebrón and comrades open fire on the US House of Representatives in the struggle for Puerto Rican independence. "I did not come to kill anyone, I came to die for Puerto Rico." —LEBRÓN, WORDS UPON ARREST

MARCH 2, 1444 Albanian resistance leader Skanderbeg founds the League of Lezhë, uniting Balkan chieftains to fight the invading Ottoman army.

THURSDAY FEBRUARY 28

Lolita Lebrón (1919–2010) following her arrest in 1954

FRIDAY MARCH 1

NOTES:

SATURDAY MARCH 2

SUNDAY MARCH 3

"Protect Students Not Guns" by Pete Railand
(Part of the Justseeds Collective's graphics portfolio)

"No Borders" by Amanda Priebe (from the Justseeds Collective's graphics portfolio)

MONDAY MARCH 4

TUESDAY MARCH 5

WEDNESDAY MARCH 6

MARCH 6, 1923 The Egyptian Feminist Union is established. "They rise in times of trouble when the wills of men are tried." —ACTIVIST HUDA SHAARAWI, *HAREM YEARS: THE MEMOIRS OF AN EGYPTIAN FEMINIST, 1879–1924*

MARCH 6, 1957 The leader of the Gold Coast's imperialism fight against the British, Pan-Africanist Kwame Nkrumah, becomes the first prime minister of independent Ghana.

MARCH 6, 1984 Coal miners walk out at Cortonwood Colliery in South Yorkshire, beginning the yearlong UK miner's strike, the longest in history. "I'd rather be a picket than a scab." —PICKET LINE SLOGAN

MARCH 7, 1921 At the Kronstadt naval base, Russia's Red Army attacks sailors, soldiers and civilians who are protesting widespread famine and the Bolshevik repression of strikes. "This unrest shows clearly enough that the party has lost the faith of the working masses." —PETROPAVLOVSK RESOLUTION AND DEMANDS

MARCH 7, 1942 Lucy Parsons, anarchist and Industrial Workers of the World cofounder who was born in slavery, dies in Chicago. "Stroll you down the avenues of the rich and look through the magnificent plate windows into their voluptuous homes, and here you will discover the *very identical robbers* who have despoiled you and yours." —"TO TRAMPS"

MARCH 8, 1914 First International Women's Day, cofounded by German Marxist Clara Zetkin, is established on this day of the year. "What made women's labour particularly attractive to the capitalists was not only its lower price but also the greater submissiveness of women."

THURSDAY MARCH 7

Lucy Parsons (1853–1942) after her arrest for rioting at a 1915 unemployment protest

FRIDAY MARCH 8

NOTES:

SATURDAY MARCH 9

SUNDAY MARCH 10

MONDAY MARCH 11

_____

_____

_____

_____

_____

_____

_____

TUESDAY MARCH 12

_____

_____

_____

_____

_____

_____

_____

_____

WEDNESDAY MARCH 13

_____

_____

_____

_____

_____

_____

_____

_____

MARCH 12, 1930 Mohandas Gandhi begins the Salt Satyagraha, challenging the British Raj. "I know the dangers attendant upon the methods adopted by me. But the country is not likely to mistake my meaning."

MARCH 13, 1933 The poet Abdukhaliq Uyghur is executed by the Chinese government for encouraging rebellion and supporting Uyghur independence.

MARCH 13, 1979 Maurice Bishop's New Jewel Movement overthrows the Grenada government, the first armed socialist revolution in a predominantly black country outside of Africa. "The true meaning of revolutionary democracy ... is a growth in fraternal love."

MARCH 14, 2008 Riots break out in Lhasa and spread throughout Tibet, targeting Han Chinese residents and businesses. "The oppressors' snipers are still standing above Tibetan people's heads; on sunny days, the beams deflected from the guns in their hands stab into the prostrating Tibetans. This is a collective memory which has been engraved on Tibetan people's hearts." **—TIBETAN POET WOESER**

MARCH 15, 1845 Friedrich Engels publishes _The Condition of the Working Class in England._

MARCH 15, 1960 A student demonstration against the fraudulent election victory of South Korean strongman Syngman Rhee was attacked by police. One month later, the body of student protester Kim Ju-yul washed ashore, his skull split open by a tear-gas grenade. The public outrage would eventually result in the April Revolution, which would end Rhee's rule.

THURSDAY MARCH 14

Abdukhaliq Uyghur, Uyghur poet

FRIDAY MARCH 15

NOTES:

SATURDAY MARCH 16

SUNDAY MARCH 17

MONDAY MARCH 18

_____

_____

_____

_____

_____

_____

TUESDAY MARCH 19

_____

_____

_____

_____

_____

_____

WEDNESDAY MARCH 20

_____

_____

_____

_____

_____

_____

_____

MARCH 18, 1871 Paris Commune is established, a participatory workers' democracy. "Workers, make no mistake—this is an all-out war, a war between parasites and workers, exploiters and producers." —COMMUNARDS, "DECLARATION BY THE CENTRAL COMMITTEE OF THE NATIONAL GUARD"

MARCH 19, 2005 First road blockade in Kennedy Road settlement in Durban, South Africa, that would become the Abahlali baseMjondolo ("shack dwellers") movement.

MARCH 21, 1960 South African police kill sixty-nine protesters in the Sharpeville Massacre, forcing the anti-apartheid movement underground.

MARCH 23, 1918 Avant-garde artist Tristan Tzara issues the Dada Manifesto, a politico-artistic movement whose anti-bourgeois stance would influence the Situationists and the Beats. "DADA DADA DADA—the roar of contorted pains, the interweaving of contraries and all contradictions, freaks and irrelevancies: LIFE."

MARCH 23, 1931 Revolutionary Bhagat Singh, who threw a bomb into India's central legislative assembly, is hanged by the British Raj. "Let me tell you, British rule is here not because God wills it but because they possess power and we do not dare to oppose them." —"WHY AM I AN ATHEIST?"

MARCH 24, 1980 Oscar Romero, archbishop of San Salvador in El Salvador and critic of the Salvadorean death squads, is assassinated while giving mass. "We are your people. The peasants you kill are your own brothers and sisters."

MARCH 24, 1987 First demonstration of ACT UP, pioneering direct-action AIDS organization, on Wall Street to protest Food and Drug Administration inaction on drug development. "Silence = Death" —ACT UP LOGO

THURSDAY MARCH 21

FRIDAY MARCH 22

SILENCE=DEATH

The iconic poster of ACT UP, 1987

NOTES:

SATURDAY MARCH 23

SUNDAY MARCH 24

MONDAY MARCH 25

MARCH 27, 1969 First national Chicano Youth Conference is hosted in Denver by Crusade for Justice, the civil rights organization founded by former boxer Corky Gonzáles.

> "I have come a long way to nowhere,
>   unwillingly dragged by that
>   monstrous, technical,
>   industrial giant
>   called
>   Progress
>   and Anglo success ..."
> —GONZÁLES, "I AM JOAQUIN"

TUESDAY MARCH 26

MARCH 29, 1942 The Hukbalahap (Philippine communist guerrilla organization) is founded; its insurgency against the government lasts eight years. "Our friends in Manila refer to us as being 'outside.' That is incorrect terminology ... We are on the inside of the struggle." —PEASANT LEADER LUIS TARUC, *BORN OF THE PEOPLE*

MARCH 30, 1892 Freethinker Robert Ingersoll, favorite orator of Walt Whitman, delivers a eulogy for the poet after his death. "Whoever produces anything by weary labor, does not need a revelation from heaven to teach him that he has a right to the thing produced." —INGERSOLL, "SOME MISTAKES OF MOSES"

WEDNESDAY MARCH 27

THURSDAY MARCH 28

Rodolfo "Corky" Gonzáles, Mexican American boxer, poet, and political activist

FRIDAY MARCH 29

NOTES:

SATURDAY MARCH 30

SUNDAY MARCH 31

V

THE GENERAL ELECTION AND ITS AFTERMATH
HEATHER GAUTNEY

The theme of 2016 was the indictment of party elites on both sides of the aisle, who had more in common with each other than they did with their own respective bases. The emerging electoral power of anti-elite forces in the United States was in part foreshadowed by the ousting of House majority leader Eric Cantor during the Virginia primary in 2014 by obscure Tea Party professor David Brat. Brat's low-budget campaign framed Cantor as out of touch with his base and in cahoots with rich businessmen like Mark Zuckerberg to outsource American jobs. By playing the class card with populist fervor, and playing to the reactionary passions and insecurities of a recession-battered people, he unseated a seven-term incumbent next in line for speaker of the house. Donald Trump seized that baton in 2016, and he ran with it.

Bernie's populism was rooted in a profoundly different kind of anti-elitism that drew masses of young people in search of a more tolerant and egalitarian future, against the jobless, debt-ridden one that the Clinton–Wall Street alliance offered. Despite early and glaring warning signs, Clinton's campaign

remained remarkably blind to the political reality that class anxieties and anti-liberalism were influencing the mood of the election, as was a yearning, especially among young people, for a trustworthy and charismatic savior.

Hillary won the popular vote by almost 3 million votes. But she did not win the race. Her campaign cited a diversity of culprits—from

"POWERFUL AND INSIGHTFUL." — CORNEL WEST

CRASHING THE PARTY

FROM THE BERNIE SANDERS CAMPAIGN TO A PROGRESSIVE MOVEMENT

HEATHER GAUTNEY

FOREWORD BY ADOLPH REED, JR.

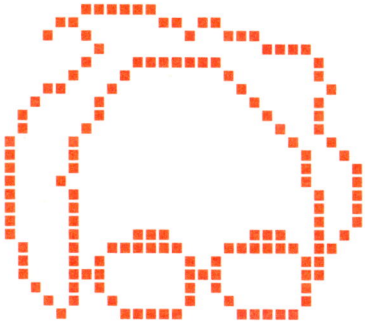

Bernie to James Comey to Vladimir Putin—as well as racism and misogyny among white Trump voters. Comey's eleventh-hour intervention *did* help tank her in the polls. And the Russian hacks and email leaks *did* paint a sordid picture of a conniving political team so obsessed with winning they'd exploit the tragedies of Sandy Hook—and so tone-deaf to the class war around them, they'd scheme to help Trump win the nomination because they thought he'd be easier to beat.

But what's important to consider for the sake of moving forward is that, like Clinton's neoliberalism, Trumpism does not offer a viable framework for unifying various segments of the population. Nor does it offer a means for addressing the higher education crisis, the sending of US jobs offshore, permanent war and climate change, widespread economic insecurity, and the lack of affordable health care. Trump may have put liberals, progressives, and the Left on the defensive, but he also left a gaping hole for a more diverse and class-conscious political movement to emerge and to offer real solutions to the most pressing issues of our time.

One critical lesson of 2016 regards the question of how to build movements and political organizations capable of confronting persistent problems of race, gender, and class inequality in America. Neoliberals on the side of Clinton patently rejected the idea that racial and gender-based injustice could be alleviated through universal forms of public investment. Instead they offered individual inclusion and mobility in consumer society as a solution—and let capital off the hook.

If Democrats are genuinely interested in mitigating racial and gender disparities in the country, they will have to start considering these disparities in terms of the structural dynamics of the larger political economy. That means implicating the fundamentals of contemporary capitalism—profit motives, global finance, and ruling class power—and the racial and gender ideologies that help legitimize them.

This is a revised extract from Heather Gautney's Crashing the Party: From the Bernie Sanders Campaign to a Progressive Movement *(Verso, 2018).*

MONDAY APRIL 1

_____
_____
_____
_____
_____
_____
_____
_____

TUESDAY APRIL 2

_____
_____
_____
_____
_____
_____
_____

WEDNESDAY APRIL 3

_____
_____
_____
_____
_____
_____
_____
_____

APRIL 1, 1649 Poor farmers begin digging plots at Saint George's Hill in Surrey, in one of the first acts of the Digger movement that sought to abolish property and wages, in some instances by occupying common land. "We are resolved to be cheated no longer, nor be held under the slavish fear of you no longer, seeing the Earth was made for us, as well as for you." —MOVEMENT FOUNDER GERRARD WINSTANLEY, "DECLARATION FROM THE POOR OPPRESSED PEOPLE OF ENGLAND"

APRIL 3, 1874 Wong Chin Foo, publisher of the first Chinese American newspaper, is naturalized as a US citizen. "The difference between the heathen and the Christian is that the heathen does good for the sake of doing good."

APRIL 3, 1895 Playwright and essayist Oscar Wilde goes on trial for homosexual activity and is imprisoned for two years. "It is immoral to use private property in order to alleviate the horrible evils that result from the institution of private property." —"THE SOUL OF MAN UNDER SOCIALISM"

APRIL 4, 1968 Martin Luther King, Jr. is assassinated. "A true revolution of values will soon look uneasily on the glaring contrast of poverty and wealth." —"BEYOND VIETNAM: A TIME TO BREAK SILENCE"

APRIL 5, 1971 The "Manifesto of the 343," signed by 343 women (including Simone de Beauvoir) who had had secret abortions, demands that the French government legalize the procedure. "These women are veiled in silence. I declare that I am one of them."

APRIL 5, 1976 On the traditional day of mourning, thousands of Beijingers lay wreaths and poems on Tiananmen Square, indirectly criticizing the Cultural Revolution.

"If a thousand challengers lie beneath your feet,
Count me as number thousand and one."

—BEI DAO, "THE ANSWER," WHICH BECAME AN ANTHEM OF THE DEMOCRACY MOVEMENT

THURSDAY APRIL 4

Dr. Martin Luther King, Jr. (1929–1968) being arrested in 1956 during the Montgomery Bus Boycott

FRIDAY APRIL 5

NOTES:

SATURDAY APRIL 6

SUNDAY APRIL 7

MONDAY APRIL 8

TUESDAY APRIL 9

WEDNESDAY APRIL 10

APRIL 8, 1950 Imprisoned for sedition, the revolutionary Turkish poet Nazim Hikmet launches a hunger strike for amnesty for political prisoners.

"Galloping from farthest Asia
    and jutting into the Mediterranean
    like a mare's head
    this country is ours."
    —**"INVITATION"**

APRIL 10, 1919 Emiliano Zapata, Mexican Revolution leader, is assassinated by the government. "The nation is tired of false men and traitors who make promises like liberators and who on arriving in power forget them and constitute themselves as tyrants."

APRIL 11, 1981 Riots break out in the Caribbean London neighborhood of Brixton in response to police targeting of young black men under the Sus law. The fighting lasts for three days.

APRIL 11, 2007 Kurt Vonnegut, author of novels with anti-authoritarian and anti-war themes, dies.

APRIL 13, 1635 Fakhr al-Din II, Druze independence leader against the Ottoman Empire and Lebanon's first freedom fighter, is executed. "No promise of reward or threat of punishment will dissuade us." —**MESSAGE TO THE PEOPLE**

APRIL 14, 1428 Vietnamese forces are victorious after a ten-year rebellion against their Chinese rulers. "Today it is a case of the grasshopper pitted against the elephant. But tomorrow the elephant will have its guts ripped out." —**REBELLION LEADER LÊ LƠI'S VICTORY SPEECH**

APRIL 14, 2002 Venezuelan president Hugo Chávez, who described his socialist movement as the Bolivarian Revolution, returns to power after having been ousted in a US-backed coup two days earlier. "What we now have to do is define the future of the world. Dawn is breaking out all over." —**ADDRESS TO THE UN GENERAL ASSEMBLY**

THURSDAY APRIL 11

FRIDAY APRIL 12

The Brixton Riots, 1981

NOTES:

SATURDAY APRIL 13

SUNDAY APRIL 14

MONDAY APRIL 15

_____

_____

_____

_____

_____

_____

_____

TUESDAY APRIL 16

_____

_____

_____

_____

_____

_____

_____

WEDNESDAY APRIL 17

_____

_____

_____

_____

_____

_____

_____

APRIL 15, 1936 The Great Revolt begins in Palestine against British Mandate and Zionism, lasting three years. "They stepped all over us until we couldn't take any more. This went on until the rebellion was smashed." —MAHMOUD ABOU DEEB, WITNESS TO THE REVOLT

APRIL 17, 1965 Protesters march against the Vietnam War in Washington DC, organized by the Students for a Democratic Society (SDS). "We must name that system. We must name it, describe it, analyze it, understand it and change it. For it is only when that system is changed and brought under control that there can be any hope for stopping the forces that create a war in Vietnam today or a murder in the South tomorrow." —SDS PRESIDENT PAUL POTTER

APRIL 18, 1955 Twenty-nine newly independent African and Asian countries meet at the Bandung Conference in Indonesia, in a show of strength for the Non-Aligned Movement. "Without peace, our independence means little." —OPENING SPEECH BY INDONESIAN LEADER SUKARNO

APRIL 20, 1773 Peter Bestes and others deliver a petition for freedom "in behalf of our fellow slaves" to the Massachusetts legislature. "The divine spirit of freedom seems to fire every human breast on the continent, except such as are bribed to assist in executing the execrable plan."

APRIL 21, 1913 The Indian revolutionary group, the Ghadar Party, is formed by Punjabis in North America. "The nation-state may truly be compared to the dinosaurs and the tyrannosaurus of the Mesozoic Age. Like those gigantic reptiles, the modern nation-state has a very small brain with which to think and plan, but tremendously powerful teeth with which to tear and rend, to destroy and dismember." —FOUNDER LALA HAR DAYAL, "HINTS OF SELF-CULTURE"

THURSDAY APRIL 18

Palestinian Arabs meet at Abu Ghosh during the Great Revolt, 1936

FRIDAY APRIL 19

NOTES:

SATURDAY APRIL 20

SUNDAY APRIL 21

MONDAY APRIL 22

_____
_____
_____
_____
_____
_____
_____
_____
_____

TUESDAY APRIL 23

_____
_____
_____
_____
_____
_____
_____
_____

WEDNESDAY APRIL 24

_____
_____
_____
_____
_____
_____
_____
_____

APRIL 22, 1977 Kenyan activist Wangari Maathai founds the Green Belt Movement, an environmental nonprofit aimed at empowering poor, rural women. "Until you dig a hole, you plant a tree, you water it and make it survive, you haven't done a thing."

APRIL 23, 1968 Students occupy buildings in New York's Columbia University to protest the school's ties to a defense contractor, triggering a campus-wide strike. "Up against the wall, Motherfuckers!" —PROTEST GRAFFITI

APRIL 24, 1916 Irish republicans mount an armed insurrection against the British imperialists on Easter week, in what became known as the Easter Rising.

APRIL 25, 1974 Portuguese armed forces overthrow the ruling Estado Novo dictatorship in what becomes known as the Carnation Revolution, setting the stage for its colonies to achieve independence.

APRIL 26, 1937 The Basque town of Guernica is destroyed in an aerial bombing by German and Italian forces, in one of the most sordid episodes of the Spanish Civil War.

"Faces good in firelight good in frost
Refusing the night the wounds and blows."
—SURREALIST POET PAUL ELUARD, "VICTORY OF GUERNICA"

APRIL 28, 1967 Heavyweight champion boxer Muhammad Ali refuses induction into the US Armed Forces, leading to a charge for draft evasion and being stripped of his titles. "I ain't got no quarrel with them Vietcong. No Vietcong ever called me nigger."

THURSDAY APRIL 25

Boxer and conscientious objector Muhammad Ali in 1966

FRIDAY APRIL 26

NOTES:

SATURDAY APRIL 27

SUNDAY APRIL 28

V

CLIMATE AND TECHNOLOGY
JAMES BRIDLE

Contemporary information networks are both the economic and cognitive frameworks of society: So how will they fare in an era of climate change? And what damage are they doing in the present?

Rising global temperatures will particularly stress data infrastructures that already run hot, as well as the people who work in and around them. Data centres and individual computers generate vast amounts of waste heat, and require corresponding quantities of cooling, from the acres of air conditioning systems on industrial buildings to the fans that cool your laptop when a YouTube kitten video sends the CPU into overdrive. Increased air temperatures bring increased cooling costs—and the possibility of outright failures. 'IPhone needs to cool down before you use it' pleads the error message on Apple's latest phone when the ambient temperature rises above forty-five degrees Celsius. Such a response can be triggered by leaving the device in a hot car in Europe today, but is projected to become a daily occurrence in the Gulf regions in the second half of the twenty-first century,

following record-breaking heat waves in 2015, when Iraq, Iran, Lebanon, Saudi Arabia and the Emirates endured daytime temperatures approaching fifty degrees Celsius.

A report on ICT and the climate written by AEA identifies a number of specific effects that will be felt by information networks. At the level of physical infrastructure, it notes that much of this network is parasitic upon structures that were not designed for their contemporary uses, nor for the effects of climate change: mobile phone masts grafted onto church steeples, data centres in old industrial units, telephone exchanges constructed in Victorian post offices. Below the ground, fibre-optic cables run through sewage channels that are becoming incapable of handling increased storm surges and flooding; cable landing sites, where the internet comes ashore from undersea data links, are susceptible to rising sea levels, which will be particularly destructive in southeast and eastern England, sites of crucial connections to the continent. Coastal installations will be increasingly susceptible to saline corrosion,

while towers and transmission masts will buckle and fall as the ground, attacked by drought and flood, shears and subsides.

In the electromagnetic spectrum, the strength and efficacy of wireless transmission will be reduced as temperatures rise. The refractive index of the atmosphere is highly dependent on humidity and severely affects the curvature of electromagnetic waves, along with the rate at which they fade. Increased temperatures and rainfall will shift the beams of point-to-point data links—such as microwave transmissions—and attenuate broadcast signals. As the earth warms and becomes wetter, ever-greater densities of wireless masts will be required, and maintenance will become more difficult. Changing types of vegetation may also impact the propagation of information.

Wi-Fi, in short, will get worse, not better. In one scenario, the shifting ground may even reduce the reliability of reference data for telecommunication and satellite transmission calculations. Accuracy falls; broadcasts overlap and interfere; noise crowds out the signal. The systems we have built to collapse time and space are being attacked by space and time.

As digital culture becomes faster, higher bandwidth, and more image-based, it also becomes more costly and destructive—both literally and figuratively. It requires more input and energy, and affirms the supremacy of the image—the visual representation of data—as the representation of the world. But these images are no longer true, and none less so than our image of the future. As the past melts into the permafrost, so is the future rocked by the atmosphere. The changing climate shakes not merely our expectations, but our ability to predict any future at all.

This is a revised extract from New Dark Age: Technology, Knowledge and the End of the Future *by James Bridle (Verso, 2018).*

MONDAY APRIL 29

TUESDAY APRIL 30

WEDNESDAY MAY 1

APRIL 29, 1992 Los Angeles residents begin rioting after the four police officers accused of beating Rodney King are acquitted. "Give us the hammer and the nails, we will rebuild the city." —BLOODS AND CRIPS, "PLAN FOR THE RECONSTRUCTION OF LOS ANGELES"

MAY 1, 1949 Albert Einstein publishes "Why Socialism?" in the inaugural issue of *Monthly Review*. "The economic anarchy of capitalist society as it exists today is, in my opinion, the real source of the evil."

MAY 1, 1970 Lesbian activists deliver their manifesto at the Second Congress to Unite Women in New York City, to protest the exclusion of lesbian speakers. "Lesbian is a label invented by the man to throw at any woman who dares to be his equal." —RADICALESBIANS, "THE WOMAN-IDENTIFIED WOMAN"

MAY 3, 1968 French students protest the closure of the Sorbonne, setting off the May '68 wave of demonstrations and strikes by millions of students and workers. "Be realistic, demand the impossible." —PARIS GRAFFITI

MAY 4, 1886 At a rally for the eight-hour day at Haymarket Square in Chicago, a bomb is thrown at police and eight anarchists are later convicted of conspiracy. "I repeat that I am the enemy of the 'order' of today, and I repeat that, with all my powers, so long as breath remains in me, I shall combat it." —LOUIS LINGG'S TRIAL SPEECH

MAY 4, 1919 Chinese students demonstrate in Beijing, sparking the anti-Confucian New Culture Movement. "Wanting to eat men, at the same time afraid of being eaten themselves, they all eye each other with the deepest suspicion." —LU XUN, *A MADMAN'S DIARY*, ONE OF THE MOVEMENT'S REPRESENTATIVE WORKS

MAY 5, 1938 Second and final arrest of Russian poet Osip Mandelstam, for writing critically of Stalin.

"He forges decrees in a line like horseshoes
One for the groin, one the forehead, temple, eye"
—"THE STALIN EPIGRAM"

THURSDAY MAY 2

FRIDAY MAY 3

The first flier calling for a rally in the Haymarket on May 4, 1886

NOTES:

SATURDAY MAY 4

SUNDAY MAY 5

MONDAY MAY 6

_____

_____

_____

_____

_____

_____

_____

_____

TUESDAY MAY 7

_____

_____

_____

_____

_____

_____

WEDNESDAY MAY 8

_____

_____

_____

_____

_____

_____

_____

MAY 9, 1918 Scottish revolutionary John Maclean, on trial for sedition for opposing WWI, delivers a rousing speech from the dock. "I am here as the accuser of capitalism, dripping with blood from head to foot."

MAY 11, 1930 Pedro Albizu Campos is elected president of the Puerto Rican Nationalist Party. "The empire is a system. It can wait. It can fatten its victims to render its digestion more enjoyable at a later time."

MAY 10, 1857 Rebellion against British rule in India begins, eventually growing into the First Indian War of Independence.

MAY 10, 1872 Victoria Woodhull, suffragist and publisher of the first English edition of _The Communist Manifesto_, becomes the first woman nominated for president of the US.

MAY 11, 1894 Three thousand employees of the Pullman railcar company go on strike, eventually growing to 250,000 workers before being crushed by federal troops.

MAY 12, 1916 James Connolly is tied to a chair and shot by the British government for his role in the Easter Rising—the precursor to the declaration of the Irish Republic in 1919. Born in Scotland to Irish immigrant parents, Connolly became a leader of the socialist movement in Scotland, Ireland and the United States, where he was a member of the Socialist Party and the IWW.

THURSDAY MAY 9

Proclamation of the Irish Republic, Easter 1916

FRIDAY MAY 10

NOTES:

SATURDAY MAY 11

SUNDAY MAY 12

MONDAY MAY 13

TUESDAY MAY 14

WEDNESDAY MAY 15

MAY 13, 1968 French workers join students in a one-day strike, with over a million protesters marching through Paris streets. By the following week, two-thirds of France's workforce was on strike, becoming the largest general strike that had ever stopped the economy of an industrialized country.

MAY 16, 1943 Warsaw Ghetto Uprising, which began in German-occupied Poland to resist the last deportation of Jews to the Treblinka extermination camp, ends in failure. "We decided to gamble for our lives." **—MAREK EDELMAN, MEMBER OF THE JEWISH COMBAT ORGANIZATION**

MAY 17, 1649 A mutiny in the New Model Army of England by the Levellers, who called for the expansion of suffrage, religious toleration, and sweeping political reforms, is crushed when its leaders are executed. "We do now hold ourselves bound in mutual duty to each other to take the best care we can for the future to avoid both the danger of returning into a slavish condition and the chargeable remedy of another war." **—LEVELLERS, "AGREEMENT OF THE PEOPLE"**

MAY 18, 1980 Citizens of Kwangju, South Korea, seize control of their city, demanding democratization, an end to martial law, and an increase in the minimum wage.

MAY 19, 1863 US president Ulysses S. Grant issues the National Eight Hour Law Proclamation, an early but symbolic victory for the struggle over the working day in the US. "Think carefully of the difference between the operative and the mechanic leaving his work at half-past seven (after dark, the most of the year), and that of the more leisurely walk home at half-past four p.m., or three hours earlier." **—MACHINIST-TURNED-ACTIVIST IRA STEWARD, "THE EIGHT HOUR MOVEMENT"**

MAY 19, 1946 Millions of Japanese take part in the Food May Day demonstrations, protesting the country's broken food delivery system.

THURSDAY MAY 16

FRIDAY MAY 17

Children participating in the protest known as Food May Day for food supplies in Japan, 1946

NOTES:

SATURDAY MAY 18

SUNDAY MAY 19

MONDAY MAY 20

TUESDAY MAY 21

WEDNESDAY MAY 22

MAY 21, 1833 William Apess, preacher, politician and descendant of the Wampanoag King Phillip, joins the Mashpee in Massachusetts in revolt against colonial abuses. "I cast my eye upon that white skin, and if I saw those crimes written upon it, I should enter my protest against it immediately and cleave to that which is more honorable."

MAY 21, 1998 Suharto resigns as president of Indonesia after three decades of authoritarian rule. "If proposals are rejected without consideration, voices silenced, criticism banned for no reason, accused of subversion and disturbing the peace, then there is only one word: resist!"
—"WARNING," WHOSE AUTHOR WIJI THUKUL DISAPPEARED AFTER PARTICIPATING IN ANTI-GOVERNMENT PROTESTS IN 1996

MAY 24, 1798 The Society of United Irishmen, a republican group influenced by the American and French revolutions, rises up against English rule in what becomes the Irish Rebellion.

"A wet winter, a dry spring
A bloody summer, and no King."
—IRISH SAYING

MAY 25, 1899 Bengal's "rebel poet" Kazi Nazrul Islam is born.

"And I shall rest, battle-weary rebel, only on the day
when the wails of the oppressed shall not rend the air and sky."
—"THE REBEL"

THURSDAY MAY 23

Demonstrations and riots against Suharto, May 1998

FRIDAY MAY 24

NOTES:

SATURDAY MAY 25

SUNDAY MAY 26

MONDAY MAY 27

_____

_____

_____

_____

_____

_____

TUESDAY MAY 28

_____

_____

_____

_____

_____

_____

WEDNESDAY MAY 29

_____

_____

_____

_____

_____

_____

_____

MAY 28, 1913 Six hundred black women march through Bloemfontein, South Africa to protest the law requiring them, as non-white workers, to carry proof of employment.

"Too long have they submitted
to white malignity;
No passes they would carry
but assert their dignity."
—POEM INSPIRED BY THE EVENT, SIGNED "JOHNNY THE OFFICE BOY"

MAY 28, 1918 First Republic of Armenia is declared, following the Armenian Resistance of 1914–18, in which between 600,000 and 1.5 million Armenians were killed by Ottoman forces.

MAY 29, 1851 Sojourner Truth, abolitionist speaker, delivers her famous "Ain't I a Woman" speech to the Women's Convention in Akron, Ohio. "I can't read, but I can hear. I have heard the Bible and I learned that Eve caused man to sin. Well, if woman upset the world, do give her a chance to set it right again."

MAY 29, 1963 Peruvian revolutionary Hugo Blanco is captured after leading a "Land or Death" peasant uprising that sparked the country's first agrarian reform. Blanco was spared from execution thanks to pleas from Bertrand Russell, Jean-Paul Sartre, Simone de Beauvoir, Che Guevara, and others. "To be a revolutionary is to love the world, to love life, to be happy." —"TO MY PEOPLE," WRITTEN FROM EL FRONTÓN PENAL COLONY

MAY 30, 1381 British peasants revolt after the Black Death and the Hundred Years' War with France.

"When Adam delved and Eve span,
Who was then the gentleman?"
—SERMON FROM JOHN BALL, AN ENGLISH PRIEST WHO GAVE VOICE TO THE REBELS' COMPLAINTS.

THURSDAY MAY 30

Armenian Revolutionary Federation fighters, banner reading
"Liberty or Death"

FRIDAY MAY 31

NOTES:

SATURDAY JUNE 1

SUNDAY JUNE 2

2

DISCOVERY DOCK, E14   £900 p/w
● Luxury three bedroom apartment
● Brand new development
● On-site leisure facilities
● Balcony overlooking the Dock
● Very short walk to Canary Wharf
Contact Canary Wharf office on 020 7515 1575

"Cities, like dreams, are made of desires and fears
even if the thread of their discourse is secret, their
rules are absurd, their perspectives deceitful and
everything conceals something else."
Italo Calvino Invisible Cities.

Laura Oldfield Ford, *Savage Messiah* (Verso, 2018)

MONDAY JUNE 3

_____

_____

_____

_____

_____

_____

_____

_____

TUESDAY JUNE 4

_____

_____

_____

_____

_____

_____

_____

_____

WEDNESDAY JUNE 5

_____

_____

_____

_____

_____

_____

_____

_____

JUNE 4, 1450 Jack Cade, who led 5,000 peasants through London, capturing and beheading King Henry VI's associates, issues a manifesto of grievances.

JUNE 4, 1920 The republican-socialist Jangal movement forms the short-lived Persian Soviet Socialist State in the Gilan province of Iran. "By the will of the working people, Soviet power has been organized in Persia." —LETTER TO TROTSKY FROM THE REVOLUTIONARY WAR COUNCIL OF THE PERSIAN RED ARMY

JUNE 4, 1989 As army tanks roll into Beijing's Tiananmen Square, protestors join Hou Dejian in singing his popular song, "Heirs of the Dragon."

> "Enemies on all sides, the sword of the dictator.
> For how many years did those gunshots resound?"

JUNE 5, 1870 Jacob Riis immigrates to the US from Denmark, initially seeking employment as a carpenter but eventually becoming a pioneering photojournalist and New York City reformer. "I believe that the danger of such conditions as are fast growing up around us is greater for the very freedom which they mock." —HOW THE OTHER HALF LIVES

JUNE 5, 1940 Novelist and Yorkshire radical J. B. Priestley broadcasts his first "Postscript" radio series for the BBC, which drew audiences of up to 16 million listeners, and was soon cancelled for being too leftist. "Britain, which in the years immediately before this war was rapidly losing such democratic virtues as it possessed, is now being bombed and burned into democracy."

JUNE 5, 2013 The _Guardian_ publishes the first batch of government documents leaked by National Security Agency whistle-blower Edward Snowden.

THURSDAY JUNE 6

Lord Saye and Sele Brought Before Jake Cade 4th July 1450
by Charles Lucy

FRIDAY JUNE 7

NOTES:

SATURDAY JUNE 8

SUNDAY JUNE 9

MONDAY JUNE 10

JUNE 10, 1952 Trinidadian historian, novelist and critic C.L.R. James is detained at Ellis Island to await deportation from the US. "The African bruises and breaks himself against his bars in the interests of freedoms wider than his own." *—A HISTORY OF NEGRO REVOLT*

JUNE 12, 1917 Founding of the Liberty League, the first organization of the "New Negro Movement" by Hubert Harrison, a black intellectual and labor leader who immigrated to the US from the US Virgin Islands.

JUNE 13, 1971 The *New York Times* publishes the first of the Daniel Ellsberg–leaked Pentagon Papers, which proved that the US government misled the public on the Vietnam War. "If the war was unjust, as I now regarded it, that meant that every Vietnamese killed by Americans or by the proxies we had financed since the 1950s had been killed by us without justification." *—SECRETS: A MEMOIR OF VIETNAM AND THE PENTAGON PAPERS*

TUESDAY JUNE 11

JUNE 15, 1813 Simón Bolívar issues his "Decree of War to the Death" for independence from Spain in Trujillo, Venezuela. "Spaniards and Canarians, count on death, even if indifferent, if you do not actively work in favor of the independence of America. Americans, count on life, even if guilty."

JUNE 16, 1971 The Polynesian Panther Party is formed in Auckland as a Maori and Pacific Islander civil rights group.

WEDNESDAY JUNE 12

THURSDAY JUNE 13

meet the representatives
of the
**POLYNESIAN
PANTHER
PARTY**
norman tuiasau
will ilolahia

Polynesian Panther Party poster, c. 1973

FRIDAY JUNE 14

NOTES:

SATURDAY JUNE 15

SUNDAY JUNE 16

MONDAY JUNE 17

JUNE 18, 1984 British police attack picketing miners with dogs, riot gear and armored vehicles, in a pivotal event of the 1984–85 UK Miners' Strike. The Battle of Orgreave is believed to be the first use of kettling, the police tactic of deploying a large cordon of officers to surround and entrap protesters.

JUNE 19, 1977 Ali Shariati, "the ideologue of the Iranian Revolution," is assassinated by the Shah's spies in the UK. "The minds of the people are prepared. The hearts of the enslaved masses are throbbing for revolt under the curtain of secrecy. One spark will be sufficient." —"RED SHI'ISM VS BLACK SHI'ISM"

TUESDAY JUNE 18

JUNE 22, 1897 Indian anti-colonialists shoot two British officers, and independence leader Bal Gangadhar Tilak is arrested for incitement. "Swaraj [self-rule] is my birthright and I shall have it!"

JUNE 22, 1955 Historian Eric Williams founds the People's National Movement, which later ushers in independence in Trinidad and Tobago. "The history of our West Indian islands can be expressed in two simple words: Columbus and Sugar." —CAPITALISM AND SLAVERY

WEDNESDAY JUNE 19

THURSDAY JUNE 20

Ali Shariati on the Haj

FRIDAY JUNE 21

NOTES:

SATURDAY JUNE 22

SUNDAY JUNE 23

MONDAY JUNE 24

TUESDAY JUNE 25

WEDNESDAY JUNE 26

JUNE 25, 1876 Battle of Little Bighorn begins in what is now Montana, with combined Lakota, Cheyenne, and Arapaho forces beating the US 7th Cavalry. "I have robbed, killed, and injured too many white men to believe in a good peace. They are medicine, and I would eventually die a lingering death. I would rather die on the field of battle." —NATIVE LEADER SITTING BULL

JUNE 25, 1892 Ida B. Wells, civil rights activist and anti-lynching campaigner, publishes an early version of her pamphlet "Southern Horrors: Lynch Law in All Its Phases." "When the white man who is always the aggressor knows he runs as great a risk of biting the dust every time his Afro-American victim does, he will have greater respect for Afro-American life."

JUNE 27, 1905 The Industrial Workers of the World is founded in Chicago, combining Marxist and trade unionist principles. "I believe we can agree that we should unite into one great organization—big enough to take in the children that are now working; big enough to take in the black man; big enough to take in all nationalities ..." —WILLIAM "BIG BILL" HAYWOOD, "THE GENERAL STRIKE"

JUNE 27, 1880 Helen Keller, world-renowned deafblind author and speaker, is born in Alabama. "If I ever contribute to the Socialist movement the book that I sometimes dream of, I know what I shall name it: Industrial Blindness and Social Deafness." —"HOW I BECAME A SOCIALIST"

JUNE 28, 1969 Riots begin at New York City's Stonewall Inn in response to a police raid, sparking the modern gay rights movement.

JULY 2, 1809 Shawnee chief Tecumseh calls on all Indians to unite against the encroachment of white settlers on native land. "The only way to stop this evil is for all the red men to unite in claiming an equal right in the land. That is how it was at first, and should be still, for the land never was divided, but was for the use of everyone." —ADDRESS TO WILLIAM HENRY HARRISON

THURSDAY JUNE 27

Civil rights activst and suffragist Ida B. Wells (1862–1931)

FRIDAY JUNE 28

NOTES:

SATURDAY JUNE 29

SUNDAY JUNE 30

THE HONEY MUSHROOM
JENNY HVAL

That was how winter came to Aybourne: rotting seaweed dried and crumbled to frozen yarn-lumps down by the beach. From the window spot on the mezzanine I saw the car park empty and fill, then empty and fill up again, and the passengers waiting at the tram stop wearing thicker coats and more layers. The high street in town was decked with fairy lights shaped like snow crystals. But the snow didn't come, like in Norway and, from where I sat, the window frame seemed more and more like the frame around an old faded photograph: the grass outside yellowish brown, the tree trunks grey and the sky white. Even the laundry on the clotheshorse lost its colours. Once I was certain I'd seen Pym down on the road, but each time he turned toward me his face looked washed out and empty.

As winter settled in outside, we were set upon by summer inside the brewery, as if the walls separated not only the inside from the outside, but divided two different climates. On the floor grass grew along the furring. Yellow moss patches grew from the cracks in the cement. White spiders spun shining fur around the beams and, because of a spreading layer of greenish-white mould, the breadcrumbs on the kitchen counter grew into a little carpet. I tried to trim the tufts and wash away the crawling maggots, but Carral cuddled up against me, took the washcloth and the scissors from my hands, and shook her head.

"That'll just make it worse," she said. "I'll tell the landlord, they can hire people from a cleaning company. That's how we do it here."

But nothing was done, and Carral seemed fine about it. She no longer thought the insects were gross. She let an ant crawl over her hand in peace while reading Moon Lips,

had become part of the damp brewery heat. Her temporary job at Sachs & Sachs had ended, and she had not found a new one yet.

"I might travel instead," she said when I asked her what she was thinking of doing. "South. I've saved up some money." But she stayed at home and made me go to the shop and to the post office to pay our rent and electricity. She would often sit by the window on the open mezzanine, as if she was guarding the brewery and couldn't leave her station. She didn't mention her plans to travel again. But she looked after me too: more often than not, I would wake up with her body next to mine, moist and milky.

and she didn't move when one of the white spiders crawled over the hollow of her neck. She just sat there with an index finger on her lips, reading. The next time I looked up from my book and over at her, the spider was gone and her mouth half-open. I kept going to lectures, and every time I left, it felt like I crossed a threshold between dream and reality, sleep and wakefulness. Outside was cold and clear, and returning to the flat at night was like entering a vast warm cocoon. Carral seldom left anymore. Increasingly she

This is an extract from Paradise Rot, *a novel by Jenny Hval (Verso, 2018).*

MONDAY JULY 1

TUESDAY JULY 2

WEDNESDAY JULY 3

JULY 4, 1789 The Marquis de Sade is moved from the Bastille prison to Charenton, days before French revolutionaries storm it and set fire to his writings there. "No act of possession can ever be perpetrated on a free being; it is as unjust to own a wife monogamously as it is to own slaves." —"PHILOSOPHY IN THE BEDROOM"

JULY 4, 1876 Susan B. Anthony and other protesters present the "Declaration of Rights for Women" at an official celebration of the centennial of the United States. "Women's wealth, thought, and labor have cemented the stones of every monument man has reared to liberty."

JULY 4, 1967 The British Parliament decriminalizes homosexuality.

JULY 5, 1885 The Protect the King movement in Vietnam begins, following a French attack on the imperial capital of Hue, and uniting the country against French colonial rule. "Better to be sentenced once than sentenced for eternity." —COORDINATOR OF RESISTANCE IN NORTHERN VIETNAM NGUYỄN QUANG BÍCH, LETTER TO THE FRENCH

JULY 7, 1969 Redstockings, a New York–based radical Marxist-feminist group, publishes its manifesto. "Liberated women—very different from women's liberation!" —REDSTOCKINGS MEMBER PAT MAINARDI, "THE POLITICS OF HOUSEWORK"

THURSDAY JULY 4

Design proposal for a US dollar featuring Susan B. Anthony, 1978-79

FRIDAY JULY 5

NOTES:

SATURDAY JULY 6

SUNDAY JULY 7

MONDAY JULY 8

TUESDAY JULY 9

WEDNESDAY JULY 10

JULY 9, 1955 Bertrand Russell and Albert Einstein issue a manifesto condemning the stockpiling and use of nuclear weapons. "There lies before us, if we choose, continual progress in happiness, knowledge, and wisdom. Shall we, instead, choose death, because we cannot forget our quarrels?" —BETRAND RUSSELL

JULY 9, 2005 Palestinian civil society organizations call for boycott, divestment and sanctions (BDS) against Israel.

JULY 13, 1524 Thomas Müntzer, radical German theologian who became a leader in the Peasants' War of 1524 to 1525, delivers his famous "Sermon to the Princes" to Saxon nobles. "Oh, you beloved lords, how well the Lord will smash down the old pots of clay [ecclesiastical authorities] with his rod of iron."

JULY 13, 1934 Nobel Prize–winning Nigerian poet and playwright Wole Soyinka is born. Over the course of his life, Soyinka is prosecuted and jailed numerous times for his outspoken political critiques.

"Traveler you must set forth
At dawn.
I promise marvels of the holy hour."
—"DEATH IN THE DAWN"

JULY 14, 1789 An organized mob breaks into a royal armory in Paris and, newly armed, storms the Bastille, a fortress that held the monarchy's political prisoners. "One resource is left; to take arms!" —SPEECH BY JOURNALIST CAMILLE DESMOULINS

JULY 14, 1877 The Great Railroad Strike begins in West Virginia, United States, pitting thousands of railroad workers against state militias and the national guardsmen summoned to break it. "Wages and revenge." —SLOGAN

THURSDAY JULY 11

Blockade of engines at Martinsburg, West Virginia, 1877

FRIDAY JULY 12

NOTES:

SATURDAY JULY 13

SUNDAY JULY 14

MONDAY JULY 15

_____

_____

_____

_____

_____

_____

_____

_____

TUESDAY JULY 16

_____

_____

_____

_____

_____

_____

_____

_____

WEDNESDAY JULY 17

_____

_____

_____

_____

_____

_____

_____

JULY 19, 1979 Ernesto Cardenal, Liberation Theology priest and poet aligned with the Sandinistas, becomes the first minister of culture under the new revolutionary government.

> "We shall celebrate in the great squares the anniversary of the Revolution
> The God that does exist is the god of the workers."
> —PSALM ("SALMO") 43

JULY 18, 1936 Resistance fighter Buenaventura Durruti forms the "Durruti Column," the largest anarchist fighting force in the Spanish Civil War. "The bourgeoisie might blast and ruin its own world before it leaves the stage of history. We carry a new world here, in our hearts." —DURRUTI IN AN INTERVIEW THREE MONTHS BEFORE BEING KILLED

JULY 19, 1961 The Sandinista National Liberation Front (FSLN) is founded; in 1979 it will overthrow the Somoza dictatorship in Nicaragua. "Those of us who propose to wage a struggle to liberate our country and make freedom a reality must rescue our own traditions and put together the facts and figures we need in order to wage an ideological war against our enemy." —FSLN COFOUNDER CARLOS FONSECA, SPEECH IN HAVANA

JULY 20, 1925 Frantz Fanon, psychiatrist and revolutionary whose writings inspired anti-colonial movements throughout the world, is born in Martinique. "HISTORY teaches us clearly that the battle against colonialism does not run straight away along the lines of nationalism." —THE WRETCHED OF THE EARTH

THURSDAY JULY 18

Sandinistas taking a smoke break, 1987

FRIDAY JULY 19

NOTES:

SATURDAY JULY 20

SUNDAY JULY 21

MONDAY JULY 22

TUESDAY JULY 23

WEDNESDAY JULY 24

JULY 23, 1900 W. E. B. Du Bois attends the First Pan-African Congress in London, where he makes the statement later immortalized in his 1903 book *Souls of Black Folk*: "The problem of the twentieth century is the problem of the color-line."

JULY 25, 1846 Henry David Thoreau is jailed for refusing to pay taxes due to his opposition to slavery and the Mexican-American war. "Under a government which imprisons any unjustly, the true place for a just man is also a prison." —*CIVIL DISOBEDIENCE*

JULY 26, 1953 Fidel Castro leads the Cuban revolution against the US-backed dictator Fulgencio Batista with an attack on the Moncada Barracks. "Condemn me. It does not matter. History will absolve me." —CASTRO, BEFORE BEING SENTENCED FOR THE ATTACK

JULY 26, 1956 Gamal Abdel Nasser, president of Egypt, announces the nationalization of the Suez Canal. "We shall yield neither to force nor the dollar."

JULY 27, 1656 Philosopher Baruch Spinoza is excommunicated from the Jewish community in Amsterdam for heretical views. "The true aim of government is liberty." —"THEOLOGICAL-POLITICAL TREATISE"

JULY 27, 1972 Selma James, cofounder of the International Wages for Housework campaign, and Mariarosa Dalla Costa publish *The Power of Women and the Subversion of the Community*, which identified women's unwaged care work as an essential element of capitalism. "We must refuse housework as women's work, as work imposed upon us, which we never invented, which has never been paid for, in which they have forced us to cope with absurd hours, twelve and thirteen a day, in order to force us to stay at home."

JULY 28, 1794 Maximilien Robespierre, the face of the French Revolution's Reign of Terror, is guillotined without a trial. "The tyrant's trial is insurrection; his judgment is the fall of his power; his penalty, whatever the liberty of the people demands." —"AGAINST GRANTING THE KING A TRIAL"

THURSDAY JULY 25

FRIDAY JULY 26

Castro with fellow revolutionary Camilo Cienfuegos entering Havana, 1959

NOTES:

SATURDAY JULY 27

SUNDAY JULY 28

IDENTITY POLITICS
ASAD HAIDER

In 1977, the term identity politics in its contemporary form was introduced into political discourse by the Combahee River Collective (CRC), a group of black lesbian militants that had formed in Boston three years earlier. In their influential collective text "A Black Feminist Statement," founding members Barbara Smith, Beverly Smith, and Demita Frazier

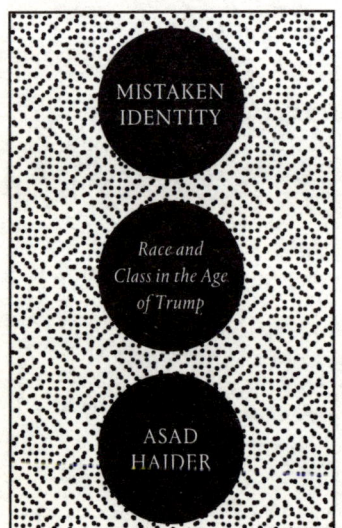

argued that the project of revolutionary socialism had been undermined by racism and sexism in the movement.

The statement brilliantly demonstrated that "the major systems of oppression are interlocking" and proclaimed the necessity of articulating "the real class situation of persons who are not merely raceless, sexless workers." Black women, whose specific social position had been neglected by both the black liberation movement and the women's liberation movement could challenge this kind of empty class reductionism simply by asserting their own autonomous politics.

As a way of conceptualizing this important aspect of their political practice, the CRC presented the hypothesis that the most radical politics emerged from placing their own experience at the center of their analysis and rooting their politics in their own particular identities. Now this did not mean, for the CRC, that politics should be reduced to the specific identities of the individuals engaged in it.

For the CRC, feminist political practice meant, for example, walking picket lines during strikes in the building trades during the 1970s. But the history that followed seemed to turn the whole thing upside down. As Salar Mohandesi writes, "What began as a promise to push beyond some of socialism's limitations to build a richer, more diverse and inclusive socialist politics" ended up "exploited by those with politics diametrically opposed to those of the CRC."

The most recent and most striking example was the presidential campaign of Hillary Clinton, which adopted the language of "intersectionality" and "privilege" and used identity politics to combat the emergence of a left-wing challenge in the Democratic Party surrounding Bernie Sanders.

I sensed that there was something unsatisfactory about politicized identity but could not quite find a way to deal with it, beyond a sort of weak dialectical ambivalence. After all, I couldn't possibly dismiss the fact that while "black faces in high places" might not mean liberation, seeing them was still profoundly meaningful for those who had suffered the psychological traumas of a racist society. Was the multicultural bourgeoisie with its ideology of identity a necessary evil—a component of the cross-class alliance that would be required to fight racism?

At times, I thought so. But as I continued to participate in social movements, I was forced to change my mind. By launching a critique of identity politics, then, I have no intention of deviating from the legacy of the Combahee River Collective or the mass movements against racism that have shaped our contemporary world. It is, rather, an attempt to deal with the contradictory reality that we cannot avoid confronting.

In its contemporary ideological form, rather than its initial form as a theorization of a revolutionary political practice, identity politics is an individualist method. It is based on the individual's demand for recognition, and it takes that individual's identity as its starting point. It takes this identity for granted and suppresses the fact that all identities are socially constructed. And because all of us necessarily have an identity that is different from everyone else's, it undermines the possibility of collective self-organization. The framework of identity reduces politics to who you are as an individual and to gaining recognition as an individual, rather than your membership in a collectivity and the collective struggle against an oppressive social structure. As a result, identity politics paradoxically ends up reinforcing the very norms it set out to criticize.

This is a revised extract from Asad Haider's Mistaken Identity: Race and Class in the Age of Trump *(Verso, 2018).*

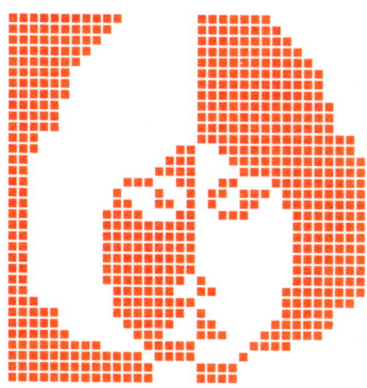

MONDAY JULY 29

TUESDAY JULY 30

WEDNESDAY JULY 31

JULY 29, 1848 The Young Irelander Rebellion of 1848 takes place: a failed Irish nationalist revolt against British rule, sometimes called the Famine Rebellion (since it took place during the Great Irish Famine) or the Battle of Ballingarry.

JULY 31, 1905 The Maji Maji rebellion begins in what is now Tanzania, led by several tribes in Tanganyika against German colonizers. "Hongo or the European, which is the stronger?" "Hongo!" —REBELLION PASSWORD

AUGUST 1, 1933 Anti-Fascist activists Bruno Tesch, Walter Möller, Karl Wolff and August Lütgens executed by the Nazi regime in Altona.

AUGUST 2, 1924 James Baldwin, black American novelist, critic, and essayist, is born in Harlem, New York City. "People can cry much easier than they can change, a rule of psychology people like me picked up as kids on the street." —"JAMES BALDWIN BACK HOME"

AUGUST 2, 1997 Fela Kuti, Nigerian father of Afrobeat and frequent presidential candidate, dies from AIDS-related complications.

AUGUST 3, 1960 Independence Day in the Republic of Niger, marking the nation's independence from France in 1960. Since 1975, it is also Arbor Day, as trees are planted across the nation to aid the fight against desertification.

THURSDAY AUGUST 1

Writer and critic James Baldwin (1924–1987)

FRIDAY AUGUST 2

NOTES:

SATURDAY AUGUST 3

SUNDAY AUGUST 4

MONDAY AUGUST 5

_____
_____
_____
_____
_____
_____
_____

TUESDAY AUGUST 6

_____
_____
_____
_____
_____
_____
_____

WEDNESDAY AUGUST 7

_____
_____
_____
_____
_____
_____
_____
_____

AUGUST 4, 1983 Revolutionary leader Thomas Sankara assumes power in Burkina Faso, nationalizing mineral wealth and redistributing land. "It took the madmen of yesterday for us to be able to act with extreme clarity today. I want to be one of those madmen. We must dare to invent the future."

AUGUST 5, 1951 Eduardo Chibas, anticommunist Cuban radio personality, shoots himself after his final broadcast. "People of Cuba, keep awake. This is my last knock at your door." —CHIBAS'S LAST WORDS

AUGUST 6, 1969 Theodor Adorno—philosopher, composer and leading member of the Frankfurt School of critical theory—dies. "For the Enlightenment, anything which cannot be resolved into numbers, and ultimately into one, is illusion; modern positivism consigns it to poetry." —_DIALECTIC OF ENLIGHTENMENT_, CO-AUTHORED WITH MAX HORKHEIMER

AUGUST 6, 2011 Riots break out throughout London after police kill a black man, lasting for several days and leading to more than 3,000 arrests.

AUGUST 8, 1961 Wu Han, a member of a dissident group of Chinese intellectuals, writes a play indirectly critical of Mao and the Great Leap Forward, for which he is imprisoned.

"You pay lip service to the principle
that the people are the roots of the state.
But officials still oppress the masses
while pretending to be virtuous men."
—"HAI JUI'S DISMISSAL"

AUGUST 9, 1650 Parliament passes an act outlawing "blasphemous" sects like the Ranters, one of the most radical to emerge during the English Revolution, which denied the authority of churches, priests, and writ.

THURSDAY AUGUST 8

Shop fire in Clapham Junction during the London Riots, August 8, 2011

FRIDAY AUGUST 9

NOTES:

SATURDAY AUGUST 10

SUNDAY AUGUST 11

MONDAY AUGUST 12

_____

_____

_____

_____

_____

_____

_____

_____

TUESDAY AUGUST 13

_____

_____

_____

_____

_____

_____

_____

WEDNESDAY AUGUST 14

_____

_____

_____

_____

_____

_____

_____

_____

AUGUST 14, 1980 Polish shipyard workers strike to protest the firing of worker Anna Walentynowicz and for the right to form unions. Walentynowicz is reinstated, and several weeks later, the first independent labor union in a Soviet bloc country, Solidarność, is formed, precipitating the fall of the Polish communist regime. "It was the end of the utopian dream, and it enabled us to dismantle the dictatorship by negotiation." —ACTIVIST ADAM MICHNIK

AUGUST 15, 1947 India becomes independent after 200 years of British colonial rule. "A moment comes, which comes but rarely in history, when we step out from the old to the new, when an age ends, and when the soul of a nation, long suppressed, finds utterance." —MOVEMENT LEADER AND INDIA'S FIRST PRIME MINISTER JAWAHARLAL NEHRU, "TRYST WITH DESTINY"

AUGUST 16, 1819 The English cavalry charges into a crowd of over 60,000 rallying in Manchester for parliamentary reform in what becomes known as the Peterloo Massacre.

"Rise like lions after slumber
In unvanquishable number!
Shake your chains to earth like dew
Which in sleep had fallen on you:
Ye are many—they are few!"
—PERCY BYSSHE SHELLEY'S "THE MASQUE OF ANARCHY," AN EARLY STATEMENT OF NONVIOLENT RESISTANCE

AUGUST 18, 1925 Mekatilili wa Menza, leader of the Kenyan Giriama people against the British Colonial Administration from 1913 to 1914, dies. "And Champion took a chick and the hen flapped and attacked him. And the Giriama said, you see what this hen has done? If you take our sons, we will do the same." —GIRIAMA TALE, IN WHICH MEKATILILI IS PERSONIFIED AS THE HEN

THURSDAY AUGUST 15

A painting of the Peterloo Massacre circulated in pro-suffrage papers, 1819

FRIDAY AUGUST 16

NOTES:

SATURDAY AUGUST 17

SUNDAY AUGUST 18

MONDAY AUGUST 19

TUESDAY AUGUST 20

WEDNESDAY AUGUST 21

AUGUST 19, 1953 Mohammad Mosaddegh, the popular, democratically elected prime minister of Iran, is overthrown by a CIA-backed coup. "My greatest sin is that I nationalized Iran's oil industry and discarded the system of political and economic exploitation by the world's greatest empire." —SPEECH AT HIS TRIAL

AUGUST 21, 1791 A rebellion against slavery breaks out in Saint Domingue, leading to the Haitian Revolution, the only slave revolt against European colonialists that successfully achieved an independent state. "We seek only to bring men to the liberty that God has given them, and that other men have taken from them only by transgressing His immutable will." —REVOLUTIONARY LEADER TOUSSAINT L'OUVERTURE

AUGUST 21, 1940 Leon Trotsky, Marxist revolutionary and theorist, is assassinated by Soviet agents. "Life is beautiful. Let the future generations cleanse it of all evil, oppression and violence, and enjoy it to the full." —"TROTSKY'S TESTAMENT," WRITTEN MONTHS EARLIER

AUGUST 21, 2013 Chelsea Manning is sentenced to thirty-five years in prison for handing off more than 700,000 government files to WikiLeaks.

AUGUST 23, 1927 During the Red Scare—a period of intense political repression in the US—the Italian-born anarchists Nicola Sacco and Bartolomeo Vanzetti are wrongfully convicted and executed for robbery and murder.

AUGUST 23, 1572 French Catholics, incited by the monarchy, kill thousands of Protestants (known as Huguenots) in the St. Bartholomew's Day Massacre, giving rise to the Monarchomachs, a movement supporting tyrannicide.

THURSDAY AUGUST 22

Attack and taking of the Crête-à-Pierrot, illustration by Auguste Raffet, 1839

FRIDAY AUGUST 23

NOTES:

SATURDAY AUGUST 24

SUNDAY AUGUST 25

MONDAY AUGUST 26

TUESDAY AUGUST 27

WEDNESDAY AUGUST 28

AUGUST 26 1789 The "Declaration of the Rights of Man and of the Citizen"—a document of the French Revolution and civil rights—is adopted by the National Constituent Assembly in France. Nicolas de Condorcet, Etta Palm d'Aelders and Olympe de Gouges called for these rights to be extended to women; Vincent Ogé, followed by the Haitian Revolution of 1791–1804, attempted to extend them to men of color and then to slaves.

AUGUST 29, 1786 Poor farmers crushed by debt and taxes rise up in armed rebellion in Massachusetts, US, in what came to be known as Shay's Rebellion. "The great men are going to get all we have and I think it is time for us to rise and put a stop to it, and have no more courts, nor sheriffs, nor collectors, nor lawyers." **—PLOUGH JOGGER, FARMER, SPEAKING AT THE ILLEGAL CONVENTION OPPOSING THE MASSACHUSETTS LEGISLATURE**

AUGUST 29, 1844 Edward Carpenter, pioneering socialist poet, philosopher, and early homosexual thinker, is born in England. "It has become clear that the number of individuals affected with 'sexual inversion' in some degree or other is very great—much greater than is generally supposed to be the case." **—HOMOGENIC LOVE**

SEPTEMBER 1, 1961 The Eritrean struggle for independence begins when members of the Eritrean Liberation Front fire first shots on the occupying Ethiopian army.

"What have I done
That you deny me my torch?"
—"SHIGEY HABUNI," POPULAR SONG WITH TIES TO THE NATIONALIST MOVEMENT

THURSDAY AUGUST 29

Declaration of the Rights of Man and of the Citizen, painted by
Jean-Jacques-François Le Barbier

FRIDAY AUGUST 30

NOTES:

SATURDAY AUGUST 31

SUNDAY SEPTEMBER 1

"Defend DACA—White House March" by Susan Simensky Bietila
(from the Justseeds Collective's graphics portfolio)

MŊÍ WIČONI

SOLIDARITY WITH STANDING ROCK

"Water is Life" by Shaun Slifer (Solidarity with Standing Rock:
Mní Wičoni is an English approximation of the Lakota "water is life."
From the Justseeds Collective's graphics portfolio)

MONDAY SEPTEMBER 2

_____
_____
_____
_____

_____
_____
_____

TUESDAY SEPTEMBER 3

_____
_____
_____
_____
_____
_____

_____
_____

WEDNESDAY SEPTEMBER 4

_____
_____

_____
_____
_____
_____
_____
_____

SEPTEMBER 2, 1945 Following two weeks of insurgency against French colonial forces, Ho Chi Minh and the Viet Minh seize control of the country and declare Vietnam independent. "Poor Indochina! You will die, if your old-fashioned youth do not resuscitate themselves." —HO CHI MINH PAMPHLET THAT BECAME THE "BIBLE OF NATIONALISTS" TWO DECADES LATER

SEPTEMBER 3, 2017 Private security guards for the Dakota Access Pipeline unleash dogs on indigenous water protectors near the Standing Rock Sioux Tribe reservation in North Dakota. A protest encampment, established months earlier, quickly swelled to become the largest gathering of Native Americans in recent history. "Mní Wičoni—Water is Life." —SLOGAN

SEPTEMBER 6, 1960 "Manifesto of the 121" is signed by French intellectuals (including Jean-Paul Sartre, Maurice Blanchot, and others), supporting the right of Algerians to fight for independence from the French. "Must we be reminded that fifteen years after the destruction of the Hitlerite order, French militarism has managed to bring back torture and restore it as an institution in Europe?"

SEPTEMBER 7, 1872 Russian revolutionary and anarchist theorist Mikhail Bakunin is expelled from the First International, presaging a split between the anarchist and Marxist factions of the workers' movement. "If you took the most ardent revolutionary, vested him in absolute power, within a year he would be worse than the Tsar himself." —BAKUNIN ON AUTHORITARIAN SOCIALISM

SEPTEMBER 8, 1965 Delano Grape Strike begins in California when Filipino grape pickers walk out and ask Cesar Chavez, leader of the mostly Latino National Farm Workers Association, to join them. The campaign ended five years later in success, largely due to a consumer boycott. "Time accomplishes for the poor what money does for the rich." —CHAVEZ, "LETTER FROM DELANO"

THURSDAY SEPTEMBER 5

Cesar Chavez (1927–1993) following the successful farmworker strike and consumer grape boycott, 1970

FRIDAY SEPTEMBER 6

NOTES:

SATURDAY SEPTEMBER 7

SUNDAY SEPTEMBER 8

MONDAY SEPTEMBER 9

TUESDAY SEPTEMBER 10

WEDNESDAY SEPTEMBER 11

SEPTEMBER 9, 869 Ali ibn Muhammad, a leader of the Zanj uprising of African slaves against the Abbasid Caliphate in Iraq, begins freeing slaves and gaining adherents. "Ali ordered their slaves to bring whips of palm branches and, while their masters and agents were prostrated on the ground, each one was given five hundred lashes." —PERSIAN HISTORIAN IBN JARIR AL-TABARI

SEPTEMBER 9, 1739 Stono Rebellion, the largest slave uprising in Britain's mainland North American colonies, led by a slave called Jemmy, erupts near Charleston, South Carolina. Over the next two years, slave uprisings occurred independently in Georgia and South Carolina, inspired by the Stono Rebellion.

SEPTEMBER 11, 1973 Salvador Allende, socialist president of Chile, bids farewell to the nation as US-backed general Pinochet carries out a coup d'etat. "I will pay for [my] loyalty to the people with my life. And I say to them that I am certain that the seeds which we have planted in the good conscience of thousands and thousands of Chileans will not be shriveled forever."

SEPTEMBER 14, 1791 Olympe de Gouges publishes the *Declaration of the Rights of Women and the Female Citizen*, one of the first tracts to champion women's rights. "Woman is born free and remains the equal of man in rights."

SEPTEMBER 15, 1889 Claude McKay, Harlem Renaissance poet and delegate to the Third International, is born in Jamaica.

"If we must die—O let us nobly die!
So that our precious blood may not be shed
In vain; then even the monsters we defy
Shall be constrained to honor us though dead!"

—"IF WE MUST DIE"

THURSDAY SEPTEMBER 12

Bombing of La Moneda (presidential palace) during the Chilean Coup of September 11, 1973

FRIDAY SEPTEMBER 13

NOTES:

SATURDAY SEPTEMBER 14

SUNDAY SEPTEMBER 15

MONDAY SEPTEMBER 16

TUESDAY SEPTEMBER 17

WEDNESDAY SEPTEMBER 18

SEPTEMBER 16, 1810 Miguel Hidalgo, a priest in Dolores, Mexico, issues a call to revolt against Spanish rule, setting in motion the Mexican War of Independence. "My children: a new dispensation come to us today. Will you receive it? Will you free yourselves?"

SEPTEMBER 16, 1923 Alongside her lover and his six-year-old nephew, Ito Noe, anarchist and feminist writer and activist, is brutally murdered by Japanese police. The event, known as the Amakasu Incident, sparked outrage throughout Japan and led to a ten-year sentence for the officer.

SEPTEMBER 16, 1973 Victor Jara, Chilean poet and songwriter, is tortured and killed in Chile Stadium following Pinochet's coup against Allende.

"How hard is it to sing
  when I must sing of horror"

— "ESTADIO CHILE," WRITTEN BY JARA IN THE STADIUM AND SMUGGLED OUT INSIDE A SHOE

SEPTEMBER 19, 1921 The Brazilian educator and philosopher Paulo Freire is born. His *Pedagogy of the Oppressed* infuses a classical theory of education with Marxist and anti-colonialist approaches. "This, then, is the great humanistic and historical task of the oppressed: to liberate themselves and their oppressors as well."

SEPTEMBER 21, 1956 Nicaraguan poet Rigoberto López Pérez assassinates Anastasio Somoza García, the longtime dictator of Nicaragua, before being killed himself. "Seeing that all efforts to return Nicaragua to being (or to becoming for the first time) a free country without shame or stain have been futile, I have decided that I should be the one to try to initiate the beginning of the end of this tyranny." —LETTER TO HIS MOTHER

THURSDAY SEPTEMBER 19

Ito Noe, Japanese anarchist and feminist

FRIDAY SEPTEMBER 20

NOTES:

SATURDAY SEPTEMBER 21

SUNDAY SEPTEMBER 22

MONDAY SEPTEMBER 23

_____

_____

_____

_____

_____

_____

_____

TUESDAY SEPTEMBER 24

_____

_____

_____

_____

_____

_____

WEDNESDAY SEPTEMBER 25

_____

_____

_____

_____

_____

_____

_____

SEPTEMBER 23, 1884 Liberal party partisans occupy a mountaintop in Kabasan, Japan, in a rebellion against the Meiji government.

> "Yet while we lament, asking
> why our insignificant selves
> were oppressed,
> the rain still falls
> heavily on the people."
> **—PARTICIPANT OHASHI GENZABURO**

SEPTEMBER 24, 1838 A meeting held on Kersal Moor in England launches the Chartist movement, the first mass working-class movement in Europe. "Our slavery has been deferred by an apprenticeship to liberty, which has aggravated the painful feeling of our social degradation, by adding to it the sickening of still deferred hope."
—THE PEOPLE'S CHARTER AND PETITION

SEPTEMBER 26, 1940 Fleeing Vichy France, Marxist theorist Walter Benjamin is threatened with deportation from Spain and kills himself with morphine tablets.

SEPTEMBER 27, 1948 Lead Belly, blues guitarist, close friend of Richard Wright's and "singing convict" who twice used his musical talents to get himself released from jail, begins recording his Last Sessions albums in New York.

> "Well, them white folks in Washington they
> know how
> To call a colored man a nigger just to see
> him bow."
> **—"BOURGEOIS BLUES"**

SEPTEMBER 28, 1829 David Walker, a contributor to the first African-American newspaper _Freedom Journal_, publishes his "Appeal to the Colored Citizens of the World," calling for slaves to revolt against their masters. Southern plantation owners respond by putting a $3,000 bounty on his head. "The whites want slaves, and want us for their slaves, but some of them will curse the day they ever saw us."

THURSDAY SEPTEMBER 26

Lead Belly (1889–1949), circa 1942

FRIDAY SEPTEMBER 27

NOTES:

SATURDAY SEPTEMBER 28

SUNDAY SEPTEMBER 29

LABOUR PAINS:
BLACK WOMEN AND WORK IN BRITAIN
BEVERLEY BRYAN, STELLA DADZIE
AND SUZANNE SCAFE

The Black woman's experience of work in Britain mirrors our experience of work over the past five centuries. This has been one long tradition of back-breaking labour in the service of European capitalism. Because it was as slaves that Black women's full labour potential was first established, and as slaves that our response to exploitation was first tested out, it is here that we begin. It was because of our ability to work that Black women were first taken as slaves from Africa to the Caribbean, and it was that same labour power which brought us from the Caribbean to Britain four hundred years later.

As Black women arriving in Britain from the Caribbean after the Second World War we were well prepared for the hard work we came here to do: our lives had been shaped and moulded by the inescapable need to find or create the work which would maintain us.

Although some black women came to Britain to join husbands who had come on ahead of them, many more came independently as recruits or simply to seek employment. A survey conducted in 1961 showed not only that the number of Black women who emigrated was equal to the number of men, but that nearly three-quarters of the women were single.

Black women were faced with no other prospect than to fill the jobs which the indigenous workforce were no longer willing to do, in the servicing, semi-skilled and unskilled sectors. Service work was little more than institutionalised housework, as night and daytime cleaners, canteen workers, laundry workers and chambermaids—an extension of the work we had done under colonialism in the Caribbean. The alternative to this was factory work in small, un-unionised sweatshops, where conditions were poor and negotiation was non-existent. On the assembly line we worked side by side with other immigrants from Asia, Ireland, and southern Europe, producing the food, clothes, shoes and goods that were so essential to Britain's post-war economic boom.

Poor working conditions were compounded by the racism we experienced at the hands of both bosses and workers. British workers felt threatened by our presence and were unable to shake off years of racist and sexist conditioning. Even though our arrival usually ensured their own promotion to less tedious and better paid sections of the industry, the fact that we were there at all was openly resented. The Race Relations Act of 1966, far from outlawing such attitudes,

merely entrenched them. The unions believed that their role was to protect the rights of the indigenous British workforce, rather than to take up and defend the rights and conditions of Black workers. The blatant racism of employers only added to our sense of alienation, and in the absence of any union protection, many of us had no choice but to accept daily harassment as a fact of life.

As women we also bore the responsibility for caring for the home and family. After working all day, we had to return home and face yet more drudgery: cooking, cleaning, washing, shopping and tending to the needs of husbands and children. Indeed, it was our children who were the most decisive factor in limiting the kinds of work we could do outside the home. Most Black women who came to Britain in the fifties and early sixties were young women who had just begun or were about to begin families. The children we left behind with aunts and grandmothers were young, too, and had to be supported. When we joined men, or were joined by them, there were more children. Contraceptives were neither free, safe nor easily available, making frequent pregnancy almost unavoidable for the majority of us. Those of our children who were born here had to be cared for, but we were no longer able to rely on other women in our families for childcare, and child-minding arrangements therefore posed a major problem for us. Local councils had no understanding of our needs and offered little or no assistance, particular

to those of us who were married to or living with a man.

In the early 1960s, the state was still busy trying to encourage (white) women to stay at home and embrace domestication and consumerism. It wasn't prepared to offer any childcare support to Black women who had to work.

This is an edited extract from The Heart of the Race: Black Women's Lives in Britain *by Beverley Bryan, Stella Dadzie and Suzanne Scafe, first published in 1985. The three authors of* The Heart of the Race *came together through their involvement in Black women's politics and through a shared commitment to reclaiming and recording Black women's struggles in Britain.*

MONDAY SEPTEMBER 30

TUESDAY OCTOBER 1

WEDNESDAY OCTOBER 2

SEPTEMBER 30, 1935 The anti-Stalinist Workers' Party of Marxist Unification (POUM) is founded in Spain, where it is especially active during the Civil War. "The totalitarian states can do great things, but there is one thing they cannot do: they cannot give the factory-worker a rifle and tell him to take it home and keep it in his bedroom. That rifle hanging on the wall of the working-class flat or laborer's cottage is the symbol of democracy." —POUM MEMBER GEORGE ORWELL, ARTICLE IN THE *EVENING STANDARD*

OCTOBER 1, 1949 Mao Zedong establishes the People's Republic of China. "A revolution is not a dinner party, or writing an essay, or painting a picture, or doing embroidery; it cannot be so refined, so leisurely and gentle, so temperate, kind, courteous, restrained and magnanimous." —"REPORT ON AN INVESTIGATION OF THE PEASANT MOVEMENT IN HUNAN"

OCTOBER 5, 1877 Nez Perce leader Hinmatóowyalahtqit, also known as Chief Joseph, ends a legendary three-month flight to Canada by surrendering to US forces. "Do not misunderstand me, but understand fully with reference to my affection for the land. I never said the land was mine to do with as I choose. The one who has a right to dispose of it is the one who created it." —"AN INDIAN'S VIEW OF INDIAN AFFAIRS"

OCTOBER 5, 1959 Robert F. Williams's Black Armed Guard fires on Ku Klux Klan members riding past a member's house in North Carolina. "Nowhere in the annals of history does the record show a people delivered from bondage by patience alone." —"WE MUST FIGHT BACK"

OCTOBER 6, 1985 Riots break out on the Broadwater Farm estate in one of London's poorest neighborhoods, a day after an Afro-Caribbean woman died of heart failure during a police search. One police officer was killed.

THURSDAY OCTOBER 3

FBI "Wanted" poster for civil rights activist Robert F. Williams (1925-1996)

FRIDAY OCTOBER 4

NOTES:

SATURDAY OCTOBER 5

SUNDAY OCTOBER 6

MONDAY OCTOBER 7

_____

_____

_____

_____

_____

_____

_____

TUESDAY OCTOBER 8

_____

_____

_____

_____

_____

_____

WEDNESDAY OCTOBER 9

_____

_____

_____

_____

_____

_____

_____

_____

OCTOBER 7, 1979 Landless farmers occupy the Macali land in Ronda Alta, Brazil, leading to the founding of the Landless Workers Movement (MST). "This is what I've always wanted: 'to overcome, to overcome.'" —MST LEADER MIGUEL ALVES DOS SANTOS

OCTOBER 8, 1969 The Weather Underground, a faction of the Students for a Democratic Society, stages the first of its "Days of Rage," a series of confrontations with the Chicago police in 1969. "Freaks are revolutionaries and revolutionaries are freaks. If you want to find us, this is where we are." —"COMMUNIQUÉ #1"

OCTOBER 10, 1837 Charles Fourier, French utopian socialist credited with inventing the word "feminism," dies after laying out his concept of utopian communities. "The extension of women's rights is the basic principle of all social progress." —"THE THEORY OF THE FOUR MOVEMENTS AND THE GENERAL DESTINIES"

OCTOBER 10, 1903 British activist Emmeline Pankhurst cofounds the Women's Social and Political Union, a militant all-women suffragist organization dedicated to "deeds, not words." "The moving spirit of militancy is deep and abiding reverence for human life." —MY OWN STORY

OCTOBER 10, 1911 The Wuchang Uprising begins after the Qing government suppresses political protest against the handover of local railways to foreign ventures. Quickly spreading through China, the Xinhai Revolution took down the 2,100-year-old dynastic empire within months.

OCTOBER 11, 1936 50,000 people visit union organizer Mother Jones's grave to celebrate her lifelong agitation on behalf of miners, establishing Mother Jones Day. "You will not be serfs, you will march, march, march on from milestone to milestone of human freedom, you will rise like men in the new day and slavery will get its death blow." —MOTHER JONES, "SPEECH TO STRIKING COAL MINERS"

THURSDAY OCTOBER 10

The two flags of the Wuchang Uprising at the birth of the Republic of China

FRIDAY OCTOBER 11

NOTES:

SATURDAY OCTOBER 12

SUNDAY OCTOBER 13

MONDAY OCTOBER 14

_____

_____

_____

_____

_____

_____

_____

TUESDAY OCTOBER 15

_____

_____

_____

_____

_____

_____

_____

WEDNESDAY OCTOBER 16

_____

_____

_____

_____

_____

_____

_____

OCTOBER 15, 1966 The Black Panther Party is founded in Oakland, California. "The people make revolution; the oppressors, by their brutal actions, cause resistance by the people. The vanguard party only teaches the correct methods of resistance." —COFOUNDER HUEY P. NEWTON, "THE CORRECT HANDLING OF A REVOLUTION"

OCTOBER 15, 1968 The Jamaican government bans the Guyanese scholar and Black Power activist Walter Rodney from the country, sparking what became known as the Rodney Riots. "The only great men among the unfree and the oppressed are those who struggle to destroy the oppressor." —HOW EUROPE UNDERDEVELOPED AFRICA

OCTOBER 17, 1961 Algerian demonstrators in Paris, denouncing France's colonial war in their home country, are met with force. An estimated 300 were massacred; the French government acknowledges forty victims.

OCTOBER 18, 1899 The Battle of Senluo Temple breaks out in northern China between government forces and the Militia United in Righteousness—known in English as the "Boxers" for their strict martial arts regimen—in what would eventually become the Boxer Rebellion, an anti-foreign and anti-Christian uprising.

"When at last all the Foreign Devils
are expelled to the very last man,
The Great Qing, united, together,
will bring peace to this our land"
—BOXERS WALL POSTER

OCTOBER 19, 1986 Samora Machel, Mozambican revolutionary leader and post-independence president, dies in a plane crash in South Africa.

THURSDAY OCTOBER 17

Black Panthers demonstrating outside of the Washington State Capitol Building, 1969

FRIDAY OCTOBER 18

NOTES:

SATURDAY OCTOBER 19

SUNDAY OCTOBER 20

MONDAY OCTOBER 21

OCTOBER 21, 1956 Dedan Kimathi, leader of Kenya's Mau Mau Uprising, is captured by a British colonial officer later nicknamed the "Butcher of Bahrain." "I lead them because God never created any nation to be ruled by another nation forever."

OCTOBER 22, 1964 Jean-Paul Sartre refuses to accept the Nobel Prize for Literature. "The writer must therefore refuse to let himself be transformed into an institution." —LETTER TO THE NOBEL COMMITTEE

OCTOBER 23, 1850 First National Women's Rights Convention meets in Worcester, Massachusetts. The following year, poet and journalist Elizabeth Oakes Smith is nominated as its president, only to be rejected after showing up in a dress baring her neck and arms. "Do we fully understand that we aim at nothing less than an entire subversion of the existing order of society, a dissolution of the whole existing social compact?"

TUESDAY OCTOBER 22

OCTOBER 23, 1856 Du Wenxiu is named Leader of All Muslims in the state established by the Panthay Rebellion, a separatist movement of the Muslim Hui people in southern China.

"They fleece sums of money,
They turn nice scenery into hell.
Alongside of extracting the land tax,
They scrape from the earth even its skin."
—DU WENXIU, WALL POSTER

WEDNESDAY OCTOBER 23

OCTOBER 27, 1967 The 1967 Abortion Act was passed in the United Kingdom, legalizing abortions for up to 28 weeks. Women in Northern Ireland continue to be excluded from access to this healthcare in their own country.

THURSDAY OCTOBER 24

Portrait of Elizabeth Oakes Smith (1806–1893), c. 1845, by John Wesley Paradise

FRIDAY OCTOBER 25

NOTES:

SATURDAY OCTOBER 26

SUNDAY OCTOBER 27

MONDAY OCTOBER 28

TUESDAY OCTOBER 29

WEDNESDAY OCTOBER 30

OCTOBER 28, 1647 The Putney Debates begin, in which members of the New Model Army, who had recently seized London, debate Britain's new constitution. "The poorest man in England is not bound in a strict sense to that government that he hath not had a voice to put himself under." —LEVELLERS SUPPORTER COLONEL RAINSBOROUGH ARGUING FOR UNIVERSAL MALE SUFFRAGE

OCTOBER 29, 1888 Li Dazhao, librarian, intellectual, and cofounder of the Chinese Communist Party, is born. "China is a rural nation and most of the laboring class consists of peasants. Unless they are liberated, our whole nation will not be liberated." —"DEVELOP THE PEASANTRY"

OCTOBER 30, 1969 The Kenya People's Union is banned, transforming the country into a one-party state; its leader, the Luo chief and first vice president of independent Kenya Oginga Odinga, is detained. "We fought for *uhuru* so that people may rule themselves. Direct action, not underhand diplomacy and silent intrigue by professional politicians, won *uhuru*, and only popular mobilization can make it meaningful." —*NOT YET UHURU*

OCTOBER 31, 1517 Martin Luther composes his letter to the Catholic Church, the *95 Theses*, which quickly spread across Europe and spark the Protestant Reformation. "He who sees a man in need, and passes him by, and gives [his money] for pardons, purchases not the indulgences of the pope, but the indignation of God."

OCTOBER 1647 Laurence Clarkson publishes *A Generall Charge*, which claimed the idea of sin was "invented by the ruling class." Clarkson was a leading Ranter, a radical sect that denied the authority of priests, churches and holy writ. "Your slavery is their liberty, and your poverty their prosperity."

THURSDAY OCTOBER 31

Chinese comintern Li Dazhao (1888–1927)

FRIDAY NOVEMBER 1

NOTES:

SATURDAY NOVEMBER 2

SUNDAY NOVEMBER 3

"WE WANT BREAD. WE ALSO WANT ROSES"
JUNO MAC AND MOLLY SMITH

Sex workers are the original feminists. In medieval Europe, brothel workers formed guilds and occasionally engaged in strikes or street protests in response to crackdowns, workplace closures or unacceptable working conditions. Fifteenth century prostitutes arraigned before the courts would answer back to their prosecutors' moralistic language by asserting that rather than a sin, their activities constituted work. In 1917, two hundred prostitutes marched in San Francisco—in what has been called "the original Women's March"—to demand an end to brothel closures. A speaker at the march declared: "Nearly every one of these women is a mother, or has someone depending on her. They are driven into this life by economic conditions ... You don't do any good by attacking us. Why don't you attack those conditions?"

Caring for each other is political work. In nineteenth-century Great Britain and Ireland, sex workers created communities of mutual aid, sharing income and childcare. An observer at the time wrote that "the ruling principle here is to share each other's fortunes ... In hard times one family readily helps another, or several help one ... What each company get is thrown into a common purse, and the nest is provisioned out of it." Sex workers in colonial-era Nairobi formed financial ties to each other, paying each others' fines or bequeathing assets to one another when they died. Although largely invisible to outsiders, this sharing of resources—including money, workspaces, and even clients—persists as a significant form of sex worker activism in the present day, with workers often collectively pitching in to prevent an eviction, or offer emergency housing. This kind of community resource sharing is often the only kind of safety net or recourse people have if they're robbed at work, or if an assault means they need time off to heal.

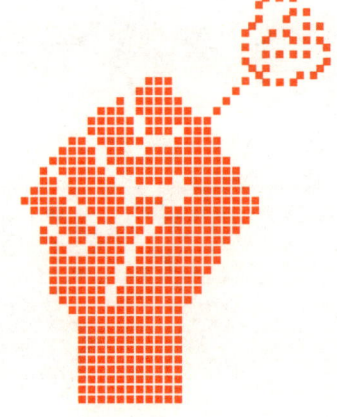

In the 1950s, sex workers were part of the Mau Mau uprising that led to Kenya's liberation from British colonial rule, and in the 1960s and 1970s LGBTQ liberation movement in the US that began with riots at Compton's Cafeteria and the Stonewall Inn. In 1974 sex workers in Ethiopia joined the newly formed Confederation of Ethiopian Labour Unions, and engaged in strike action that helped to bring down the government. Within Europe, the modern movement is generally considered to have begun in 1975, when sex workers in France occupied churches to protest criminalisation, poverty, and police violence. This sparked similar sex worker organising in the UK, and the English Collective of Prostitutes occupied churches in King's Cross, London, in 1980. More recently, sex workers were deeply involved in anti-gentrification protests around Gezi Park in Istanbul, Turkey.

The 1970s and 1980s sex workers' rights movement in the UK was deeply embedded in the 'wages for housework' campaign. This saw Marxist feminists naming the value of women's unpaid reproductive and domestic labour, and demanding a radical re-organisation of society in a way that placed value on work deemed to be women's work. Around that time, Wages Due Lesbians linked domestic work, sex work, and the work of sexuality in a solidarity statement against a 1977 vice crackdown: "Wherever women succeed in winning some of the wages due us, it is a strength to all of us and proof that women's services cannot be taken for granted."

In 2001, twenty-five thousand sex workers came to Kolkata to make their demands known. Their signs proclaimed: "We want bread. We also want roses."

This is an extract from Revolting Prostitutes: The Fight for Sex Workers' Rights *by Juno Mac and Molly Smith (Verso, 2018).*

MONDAY NOVEMBER 4

_____

_____

_____

_____

_____

_____

_____

_____

TUESDAY NOVEMBER 5

_____

_____

_____

_____

_____

_____

_____

WEDNESDAY NOVEMBER 6

_____

_____

_____

_____

_____

_____

_____

NOVEMBER 4, 1780 Quechua leader Túpac Amaru II leads an indigenous rebellion against Spanish control of Peru, beginning with the capture and killing of the Spanish governor by his slave. "There are no accomplices here but you and I. You the oppressor and I the liberator. Both of us deserve to die." **—TÚPAC AMARU II, LAST WORDS TO GENERAL JOSÉ ANTONIO DE ARECHE**

NOVEMBER 7, 1917 Lenin leads the Bolsheviks in revolution against the provisional Russian government, establishing what will become the Soviet Union. "Freedom in capitalist society always remains about the same as it was in the ancient Greek republics: freedom for the slave-owners." **—THE STATE AND REVOLUTION**

NOVEMBER 7, 1951 Philosopher Michel Foucault is a leading figure in Paris protests against the racially motivated killing of Arab immigrant Djellali Ben Ali.

NOVEMBER 8, 1775 Thomas Spence, English radical and advocate for common ownership of land, delivers a speech with one of the earliest uses of the term "Rights of Man."

"Ye landlords vile, whose man's place mar,
  Come levy rents here if you can;
  Your stewards and lawyers I defy,
  And live with all the RIGHTS OF MAN"
    —"THE REAL RIGHTS OF MAN"

NOVEMBER 10, 1995 Nigerian government hangs Ken Saro-Wiwa and the rest of the Ogoni Nine for their campaigning against the oil industry, and especially Royal Dutch Shell. "Dance your anger and your joys; dance the military guns to silence; dance their dumb laws to the dump; dance oppression and injustice to death; dance the end of Shell's ecological war of thirty years." **—STATEMENT OF THE OGONI PEOPLE TO THE TENTH SESSION OF THE WORKING GROUP IN INDIGENOUS POPULATIONS**

THURSDAY NOVEMBER 7

Lenin speaking at an assembly of Red Army troops bound for the Polish front, with Trotsky at the base, Moscow, 1920

FRIDAY NOVEMBER 8

NOTES:

SATURDAY NOVEMBER 9

SUNDAY NOVEMBER 10

MONDAY NOVEMBER 11

_____

_____

_____

_____

_____

_____

_____

TUESDAY NOVEMBER 12

_____

_____

_____

_____

_____

_____

WEDNESDAY NOVEMBER 13

_____

_____

_____

_____

_____

_____

_____

NOVEMBER 12, 1798 Father of Irish republicanism Wolfe Tone was to be executed by the British for treason, but slit his own throat before the sentence was carried out. "If the men of property will not support us, they must fall. Our strength shall come from that great and respectable class, the men of no property."

NOVEMBER 13, 1787 Thomas Jefferson, slaveholder and author of the American Declaration of Independence, endorses frequent rebellion in a letter to William Smith. "What signify a few lives lost in a century or two? The tree of liberty must be refreshed from time to time with the blood of patriots and tyrants. It is its natural manure."

NOVEMBER 13, 1792 Louis Antoine de Saint-Just, close friend and ally of Robespierre, delivers his first speech to the revolutionary National Convention in favor of executing the king. "Dare! The word contains all the politics of our revolution."

NOVEMBER 15, 1781 Túpac Katari, Aymara leader of an army that laid siege to the Spanish colonial city of La Paz, Bolivia, is betrayed and killed. "I die but will return tomorrow as thousand thousands." **—KATARI'S LAST WORDS**

NOVEMBER 15, 1988 Palestinian Declaration of Independence, written by poet Mahmoud Darwish, is proclaimed.

"O those who pass between fleeting words
Pile your illusions in a deserted pit, and be gone"

NOVEMBER 15, 2011 Occupy Wall Street, the protest camp that had occupied New York's Zuccotti Park for nearly two months, is evicted by police.

NOVEMBER 16, 1885 Louis Riel, Métis leader who headed two rebellions against a Canadian incursion into their territory, is hanged for treason. "I will perhaps be one day acknowledged as more than a leader of the half-breeds, and if I am I will have an opportunity of being acknowledged as a leader of good in this great country." **—RIEL'S FINAL STATEMENT TO THE JURY**

THURSDAY NOVEMBER 14

The leadership of the PLO during their confrontation with the King of Jordan, 1970

FRIDAY NOVEMBER 15

NOTES:

SATURDAY NOVEMBER 16

SUNDAY NOVEMBER 17

MONDAY NOVEMBER 18

_____

_____

_____

_____

_____

_____

_____

TUESDAY NOVEMBER 19

_____

_____

_____

_____

_____

_____

_____

WEDNESDAY NOVEMBER 20

_____

_____

_____

_____

_____

_____

_____

_____

NOVEMBER 19, 1915 Joe Hill, militant songwriter and organizer with the International Workers of the World, is executed by firing squad. "Don't waste any time in mourning organize." —HILL'S FAREWELL LETTER TO BILL HAYWOOD

NOVEMBER 19, 1979 Angela Davis—black feminist, philosopher, and prison abolitionist—wins the vice presidential nomination for the US Communist Party. "Prisons do not disappear problems, they disappear human beings. And the practice of disappearing vast numbers of people from poor, immigrant, and racially marginalized communities has literally become big business." —"MASKED RACISM"

NOVEMBER 20, 1969 The Native American group Indians of All Tribes occupies Alcatraz island in the San Francisco Bay and holds it for fourteen months. "Alcatraz Island is more than suitable as an Indian Reservation, as determined by the white man's own standards." —ALCATRAZ PROCLAMATION

NOVEMBER 24, 1947 House Un-American Activities Committee votes to hold the "Hollywood Ten," a group of writers and directors blacklisted for their communist affiliations, in contempt of Congress. "We are men of peace, we are men who work and we want no quarrel. But if you destroy our peace, if you take away our work, if you try to range us one against the other, we will know what to do." —SPARTACUS SCREENWRITER DALTON TRUMBO'S ANTIWAR NOVEL, JOHNNY GOT HIS GUN

NOVEMBER 24, 2014 A white police officer is acquitted in the shooting death of an unarmed black teenager, Michael Brown, in Ferguson, Missouri, setting off protests nationwide under the moniker Black Lives Matter.

THURSDAY NOVEMBER 21

Angela Davis on her first visit to the Soviet Union, 1972

FRIDAY NOVEMBER 22

NOTES:

SATURDAY NOVEMBER 23

SUNDAY NOVEMBER 24

MONDAY NOVEMBER 25

TUESDAY NOVEMBER 26

WEDNESDAY NOVEMBER 27

NOVEMBER 25, 1832 Abd al-Qader al-Jaza'iri, Sufi and Muslim scholar and Algerian resistance leader, is elected emir of a confederation of tribes that banded together and fought the French invaders for over a decade. "If we leave them alone, they will assault us."

NOVEMBER 29, 1947 The UN approves the partition of Palestine, despite its rejection by Palestinian Arabs and the fact that 90 percent of privately held land was Arab-owned.

"They've prohibited oppression among themselves
but for us they legalized all prohibitions!
They proclaim, 'Trading with slaves is unlawful'
but isn't the trading of free people more of a crime?"

—PALESTINIAN POET ABU SALMA, "MY COUNTRY ON PARTITION DAY"

NOVEMBER 30, 1999 The World Trade Organization meeting in Seattle is disrupted by massive anti-globalization protests. "When we smash a window, we aim to destroy the thin veneer of legitimacy that surrounds private property rights." —ACME COLLECTIVE, "ON THE VIOLENCE OF PROPERTY"

DECEMBER 1, 1955 Rosa Parks is arrested for refusing to give up her seat on a segregated bus, which triggers a boycott organized by the Women's Political Council of Montgomery. "Negroes have rights, too, for if Negroes did not ride the busses, they could not operate." —WOMEN'S POLITICAL COUNCIL PAMPHLET

THURSDAY NOVEMBER 28

Rosa Parks (1913–2005) being fingerprinted after her arrest for boycotting public transportation in Montgomery, Alabama, 1956

FRIDAY NOVEMBER 29

NOTES:

SATURDAY NOVEMBER 30

SUNDAY DECEMBER 1

V

WE BUILT THE WALL
EILEEN TRUAX

For decades, the United States has promoted itself to the rest of the world as a democratic country, with a policy of open arms and affirming diversity, which has very little to do with how the nation actually shapes its policies around immigration, refuge, and asylum. In spite of being the country with the largest number of immigrants in the world—almost 50 million people living in US territory were not born there—the United States has a smaller percentage of immigrants in relation to the general population than other countries. Immigrants comprise 14 percent of the US population, compared with 22 percent in Canada and 28 percent in Australia.

As with most countries that receive immigrants, the current demographic composition of the United States is the result of the government's application of immigration policy based on the country's economic and workplace needs. But it is also a function of the alliances and shifting sands of international politics. In terms of refuge and asylum policy, and the methods for detaining and processing immigrants, the predominant principles have more to do with political, and even partisan, criteria, not human rights or social justice. The United States opens its arms to whoever benefits it economically at the moment, and to asylum and refuge seekers who can demonstrate persecution or a threat to their safety or their lives, as long as they come from countries with governments viewed as questionable by the United States.

One hallmark of Donald Trump's presidential campaign was connecting anti-terrorist and national security rhetoric with migration. In addition to justifying measures like the "Muslim ban," such connections encompassed building a border wall, accusing Mexicans of

How the U.S. Keeps Out Asylum Seekers from
Mexico, Central America and Beyond

WE BUILT THE WALL

Eileen Truax

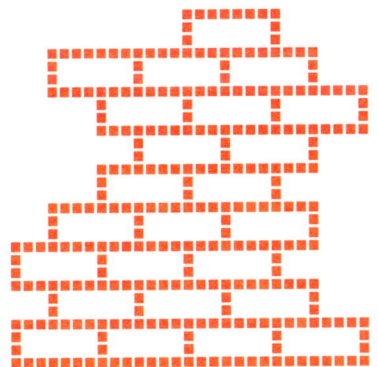

being drug dealers and rapists, and claiming without evidence that undocumented people vote illegally; these last two assertions reinforced his promise to deport 11 million undocumented people from the country.

Although talking about Trump as a dangerous threat to immigrants has been a good strategy for media outlets trying to increase their online traffic, the so-called "deportation machine" has already been up and running for at least a decade, beginning with the George W. Bush administration in 2001 in the wake of the 9/11 terrorist attacks, and picking up steam during Barack Obama's time in office. Almost 3 million people were deported in the eight years of Obama's presidency—a number that Trump has provided as a possible goal for his administration. And the criteria in place for granting refuge or asylum were established

fifty years ago, initially based on international humanitarian goals but implemented in the service of convenience and political interests.

US immigration policy during the Trump presidency and in the years beyond could be outrageous and appalling, but these politics are not new. Most Americans have refused to acknowledge that the immigrant community has endured discrimination and a hostile environment for decades. Tax dollars paid by US residents are spent to lock up immigrants, re-victimizing those who have already been victimized in their home countries, who have reached out to "the best democracy in the world" in an attempt to save their own lives. We rarely think about the new arrivals who have had to leave everything behind and come here as a last resort, arriving in a new land only to be labeled "the other," the foreigner, and whose lives depend on accepting this description. From the comfort of our own secure legal status, we have already built the Wall.

This is a revised extract from Eileen Truax's We Built the Wall: How the US Keeps Out Asylum Seekers from Mexico, Central America and Beyond, *translated by Diane Stockwell (Verso, 2018).*

MONDAY DECEMBER 2

TUESDAY DECEMBER 3

WEDNESDAY DECEMBER 4

DECEMBER 2, 1931 Folksinger and United Mine Workers activist Aunt Molly Jackson performs in the Bronx, as part of a send-off to workers leaving to participate in the National Hunger March on Washington.

> "Their banner is the dollar sign
> While ours is striped with blood."
> —"I AM A UNION WOMAN"

DECEMBER 2, 1964 Berkeley Free Speech Movement leader Mario Savio gives his famous speech on the steps of Sproul Hall. The next day, nearly 800 protesters are arrested on the UC Berkeley campus while resisting restrictions on political speech. "You've got to put your bodies upon the gears and upon the wheels ... upon the levers, upon all the apparatus, and you've got to make it stop."

DECEMBER 4, 1969 Fred Hampton, Black Panther leader, is assassinated in a raid on his apartment by the Chicago Police with the help of the FBI. "We've got to go up on the mountaintop to make this motherfucker understand, goddamnit, that we are coming from the valley!" —HAMPTON SPEECH AT OLIVET CHURCH

DECEMBER 5, 1978 Wei Jingsheng posts his manifesto "The Fifth Modernization," which was critical of the Communist leadership, to Beijing's Democracy Wall, and is imprisoned for 15 years. "Let us find out for ourselves what should be done."

DECEMBER 6, 1928 The United Fruit Company violently suppresses a worker's strike in Colombia, in what becomes known as the Banana Massacre.

DECEMBER 6, 2008 Greek police shoot and kill Alexandros Grigoropoulos, a fifteen-year-old boy, sparking three weeks of rioting, protests, and occupations around the country.

> "We are here
> we are everywhere
> we are an image from the future."
>
> —OCCUPATION STATEMENT, ATHENS SCHOOL OF
> ECONOMICS AND BUSINESS STUDENTS

THURSDAY DECEMBER 5

Rioters in Athens, 2008

FRIDAY DECEMBER 6

NOTES:

SATURDAY DECEMBER 7

SUNDAY DECEMBER 8

MONDAY DECEMBER 9

TUESDAY DECEMBER 10

WEDNESDAY DECEMBER 11

DECEMBER 9, 2002 To Huu, one of the Viet Minh's most celebrated poets, dies.

> "The ditches must go deeper than my hatred.
> The work must fly faster than my tears."
> —"GUERILLA WOMAN"

DECEMBER 10, 2008 Charter 08, a document for greater democratization, is published, signed by more than 350 Chinese writers, including poet and essayist Woeser, and human rights activist Liu Xiaobo. "The decline of the current system has reached the point where change is no longer optional."

DECEMBER 11, 1977 Moroccan poet Saida Menebhi dies in prison after a thirty-four-day hunger strike. Her work was central in the nationwide attempt to recover the history of the thousands of people who were "disappeared" in the 1970s and 1980s.

> "Prison is ugly
> you draw it my child
> with black marks
> for the bars and grills"

DECEMBER 11, 2012 Theresa Spence, Chief of Attawapiskat First Nations in Canada, begins a hunger strike that would set off the indigenous sovereignty movement Idle No More.

DECEMBER 13, 1797 Heinrich Heine, German-Jewish poet and essayist, is born. No writer would be more hated by the Nazis.

> "Ye fools, so closely to search my trunk!
> Ye will find in it really nothing:
> My contraband goods I carry about
> In my head, not hid in my clothing"
> —"A WINTER'S TALE"

DECEMBER 14, 2008 Iraqi journalist Muntadhar al-Zaidi throws his shoe at US president George W. Bush at a press conference. "This is a farewell kiss from the Iraqi people, you dog."

THURSDAY DECEMBER 12

Muntadhar al-Zaidi is pulled away after throwing his shoes at George W. Bush

FRIDAY DECEMBER 13

NOTES:

SATURDAY DECEMBER 14

SUNDAY DECEMBER 15

MONDAY DECEMBER 16

TUESDAY DECEMBER 17

WEDNESDAY DECEMBER 18

DECEMBER 16, 1656 Radical English Quaker leader James Nayler is arrested for blasphemy after reenacting Christ's entry into Jerusalem by entering Bristol on a donkey. "There is a spirit which I feel that delights to do no evil, nor to revenge any wrong, but delights to endure all things, in hope to enjoy its own in the end." **—NAYLER'S FINAL STATEMENT**

DECEMBER 17, 1830 Simón Bolívar, nicknamed "El Libertador" for leading Bolivia, Colombia, Ecuador, Panama, Peru, and his native Venezuela to independence from Spain, dies. "If my death will help to end factions and to consolidate the Union, I shall go to my grave in peace." **—A PROCLAMATION ISSUED A WEEK BEFORE HIS DEATH**

DECEMBER 18, 2010 Demonstrations begin in Tunisia, the day after street vendor Mohammed Bouazizi self-immolated in protest of harassment from officials, setting off what would eventually become the Arab Spring.

DECEMBER 19, 1944 US soldier Kurt Vonnegut becomes a Nazi prisoner of war. The experience later shapes his novels, which often explore anti-authoritarian and anti-war themes. "There is no reason goodness cannot triumph over evil, so long as the angels are as organized as the Mafia." **—CAT'S CRADLE**

DECEMBER 20, 1986 More than 30,000 students march through Shanghai chanting pro-democracy slogans. "When will the people be in charge?"

DECEMBER 22, 1964 Sam Cooke's "A Change Is Gonna Come" is released and soon becomes an anthem for the US Civil Rights Movement.

"It's been a long, a long time coming
But I know
A change gon' come."

THURSDAY DECEMBER 19

Simón Bolívar (1783–1830), painting by Arturo Michelena

FRIDAY DECEMBER 20

NOTES:

SATURDAY DECEMBER 21

SUNDAY DECEMBER 22

MONDAY DECEMBER 23

TUESDAY DECEMBER 24

WEDNESDAY DECEMBER 25

DECEMBER 23, 1986 Dissident and Nobel Peace Prize–winner Andrei Sakharov returns to Moscow after six years spent in internal exile for protesting the Soviet war in Afghanistan. "Freedom of thought is the only guarantee against an infection of people by mass myths, which, in the hands of treacherous hypocrites and demagogues, can be transformed into bloody dictatorship."

DECEMBER 25, 1831 Samuel Sharpe, leader of the Native Baptists of Montego Bay, leads Jamaican slaves in the Great Jamaican Slave Revolt, which was instrumental in abolishing chattel slavery. "I would rather die upon yonder gallows than live in slavery." —SHARPE'S LAST WORDS

DECEMBER 25, 1914 Disobeying their commanding officers, thousands of German and British soldiers organized unofficial ceasefires along the Western Front in the week leading up to Christmas, climbing out of their trenches and even exchanging gifts.

DECEMBER 25, 1927 B. R. Ambedkar, an architect of the Indian constitution who was born into the Dalit caste of "untouchables," leads followers to burn the Manusmriti, an ancient text justifying the hierarchy. The "untouchables" were relegated to occupations considered impure, like butchering and waste removal.

DECEMBER 25, 1977 Domitila Barrios de Chungara, an activist with the militant Bolivian labor group Housewives' Committee, begins a hunger strike that leads to the end of the US-backed Bolivian dictatorship. "The first battle to be won is to let the woman, the man, the children participate in the struggle of the working class, so that the home can become a stronghold that the enemy can't overcome."

THURSDAY DECEMBER 26

B. R. Ambedkar during his tenure as chairman of the committee for drafting the constitution, 1950

FRIDAY DECEMBER 27

NOTES:

SATURDAY DECEMBER 28

SUNDAY DECEMBER 29

MONDAY DECEMBER 30

TUESDAY DECEMBER 31

WEDNESDAY JANUARY 1

DECEMBER 30, 1884 William Morris, Eleanor Marx, and others establish the Socialist League, a revolutionary organization in the UK. "Civilization has reduced the workman to such a skinny and pitiful existence, that he scarcely knows how to frame a desire for any life much better." —MORRIS, "HOW I BECAME A SOCIALIST"

DECEMBER 30, 1896 José Rizal, Filipino nationalist revolutionary and writer, is executed by the Spanish on charges of rebellion, sedition, and conspiracy.

DECEMBER 31, 1977 Kenyan writer Ngũgĩ wa Thiong'o is imprisoned for cowriting a play critical of the Kenyan government.

"We the workers in factories and plantations said in one voice:
We reject slave wages!
Do you remember the 1948 general strike?"
—NGŨGĨ WA THIONG'O AND NGŨGĨ WA MIRII, *I WILL MARRY WHEN I WANT*

DECEMBER 973 Philosopher and poet Abu Ala Al-Ma'arri, a constant champion of reason against superstition, authority and tradition, is born near Aleppo, Syria.

"But some hope a divine leader with prophetic voice
Will rise amid the gazing silent ranks
An idle thought! There's none to lead but reason,
To point the morning and evening ways."

JANUARY 1, 1970 Gil Scott-Heron, the poet and recording artist who became a voice of black protest culture, releases his album *Small Talk at 125th and Lenox*, whose opening track is, "The Revolution Will Not be Televised."

"The revolution will not make you look five pounds thinner,
the revolution will not be televised, Brother."

THURSDAY JANUARY 2

Gil Scott-Heron (1949–2011)

FRIDAY JANUARY 3

NOTES:

SATURDAY JANUARY 4

SUNDAY JANUARY 5

VERSO READING LISTS

ECOLOGY AND CLIMATE CHANGE

OUT OF THE WRECKAGE:
A NEW POLITICS IN THE AGE OF CRISIS
GEORGE MONBIOT

CARBON DEMOCRACY:
POLITICAL POWER IN THE AGE OF OIL
TIMOTHY MITCHELL

FOSSIL CAPITAL: THE RISE OF STEAM POWER
AND THE ROOTS OF GLOBAL WARMING
ANDREAS MALM

GREEN GONE WRONG: DISPATCHES FROM
THE FRONT LINES OF ECO-CAPITALISM
HEATHER ROGERS

EXTREME CITIES: THE PERILS AND
PROMISE OF URBAN LIFE IN THE AGE
OF CLIMATE CHANGE
ASHLEY DAWSON

CAPITALISM IN THE WEB OF LIFE:
ECOLOGY AND THE ACCUMULATION
OF CAPITAL
JASON W. MOORE

NO WALLS, NO BORDERS

DEPORT, DEPRIVE, EXTRADITE:
21ST CENTURY STATE EXTREMISM
NISHA KAPOOR

EUROPE'S FAULT LINES:
RACISM AND THE RISE OF THE RIGHT
LIZ FEKETE

THREADS: FROM THE REFUGEE CRISIS
KATE EVANS

VIOLENT BORDERS:
REFUGEES AND THE RIGHT TO MOVE
REECE JONES

WE BUILT THE WALL: HOW THE US KEEPS OUT
ASYLUM SEEKERS FROM MEXICO, CENTRAL
AMERICA AND BEYOND
EILEEN TRUAX

HISTORY

A WORLD TO WIN:
THE LIFE AND WORKS OF KARL MARX
SVEN-ERIC LIEDMAN

TEAR GAS: FROM THE BATTLEFIELDS OF
WORLD WAR I TO THE STREETS OF TODAY
ANNE FEIGENBAUM

OCTOBER: THE STORY OF
THE RUSSIAN REVOLUTION
CHINA MIÉVILLE

REVOLUTIONARY YIDDISHLAND:
A HISTORY OF JEWISH RADICALISM
ALAIN BROSSAT AND SYLVIA KLINGBERG

THE AMERICAN CRUCIBLE: SLAVERY,
EMANCIPATION AND HUMAN RIGHTS
ROBIN BLACKBURN

A CIVIL WAR: A HISTORY OF THE
ITALIAN RESISTANCE
CLAUDIO PAVONE

LINEAGES OF THE ABSOLUTIST STATE
PERRY ANDERSON

THE DIGNITY OF CHARTISM
DOROTHY THOMPSON

**INVENTING THE FUTURE: POSTCAPITALISM
AND THE WORLD WITHOUT WORK**
NICK SRNICEK AND ALEX WILLIAMS

**STATE OF INSECURITY:
GOVERNMENT OF THE PRECARIOUS**
ISABELL LOREY

ART AND AESTHETICS

**ARTIFICIAL HELLS: PARTICIPATORY ART
AND THE POLITICS OF SPECTATORSHIP**
CLAIRE BISHOP

SAVAGE MESSIAH
LAURA OLDFIELD FORD

**ALL THAT IS SOLID MELTS INTO AIR:
THE EXPERIENCE OF MODERNITY**
MARSHALL BERMAN

PORTRAITS: JOHN BERGER ON ARTISTS
JOHN BERGER

**AISTHESIS: SCENES FROM THE AESTHETIC
REGIME OF ART**
JACQUES RANCIÈRE

CITIES AND ARCHITECTURE

**MUNICIPAL DREAMS:
THE RISE AND FALL OF COUNCIL HOUSING**
JOHN BOUGHTON

**EXTRASTATECRAFT:
THE POWER OF INFRASTRUCTURE SPACE**
KELLER EASTERLING

**EXQUISITE CORPSE:
WRITING ON BUILDINGS**
MICHAEL SORKIN

**IN DEFENSE OF HOUSING:
THE POLITICS OF CRISIS**
DAVID MADDEN AND PETER MARCUSE

**THE AUTONOMOUS CITY:
A HISTORY OF URBAN SQUATTING**
ALEX VASUDEVAN

**REBEL CITIES: FROM THE RIGHT TO THE CITY
TO THE URBAN REVOLUTION**
DAVID HARVEY

RACE AND ETHNICITY

FUTURES OF BLACK RADICALISM
EDITED BY GAYE THERESA JOHNSON
AND ALEX LUBIN

BLACK RADICAL TRADITION: A READER
EDITED BY BEN MABIE, ERIN GRAY
AND ASAD HAIDER

**IF THEY COME IN THE MORNING…:
VOICES OF RESISTANCE**
EDITED BY ANGELA Y. DAVIS

**RACECRAFT: THE SOUL OF INEQUALITY
IN AMERICAN LIFE**
KAREN E. FIELDS AND BARBARA J. FIELDS

**THE MUSLIMS ARE COMING!:
ISLAMOPHOBIA, EXTREMISM,
AND THE DOMESTIC WAR ON TERROR**
ARUN KUNDNANI

**BEYOND BLACK AND WHITE:
FROM CIVIL RIGHTS TO BARACK OBAMA**
MANNING MARABLE

FEMINISM AND GENDER

**REVOLTING PROSTITUTES:
THE FIGHT FOR SEX-WORKERS' RIGHTS**
MOLLY SMITH AND JUNO MAC

**THE HEART OF THE RACE:
BLACK WOMEN'S LIVES IN BRITAIN**
BEVERLEY BRYAN, STELLA DADZIE
AND SUZANNA SCAFE

**THE DIALECTIC OF SEX:
THE CASE FOR FEMINIST REVOLUTION**
SHULAMITH FIRESTONE

TRANS: A MEMOIR
JULIET JACQUES

**FEMINISM AND NATIONALISM
IN THE THIRD WORLD**
KUMARI JAYAWARDENA

**BLACK MACHO AND THE MYTH
OF THE SUPERWOMAN**
MICHELE WALLACE

NOTES

NOTES

NOTES